For Thou Art With Me

My Journey of Cancer through Poetry

Judith Lane Bynum

BALBOA
PRESS
A DIVISION OF HAY HOUSE

Balboa Press books may be ordered through booksellers or by contacting:

Balboa Press
A Division of Hay House
1663 Liberty Drive
Bloomington, IN 47403
www.balboapress.com
1 (877) 407-4847

Because of the dynamic nature of the Internet, any web addresses or links contained in this book may have changed since publication and may no longer be valid. The views expressed in this work are solely those of the author and do not necessarily reflect the views of the publisher, and the publisher hereby disclaims any responsibility for them.

The author of this book does not dispense medical advice or prescribe the use of any technique as a form of treatment for physical, emotional, or medical problems without the advice of a physician, either directly or indirectly. The intent of the author is only to offer information of a general nature to help you in your quest for emotional and spiritual well-being. In the event you use any of the information in this book for yourself, which is your constitutional right, the author and the publisher assume no responsibility for your actions.

Any people depicted in stock imagery provided by Getty Images are models, and such images are being used for illustrative purposes only. Certain stock imagery © Getty Images.

Print information available on the last page.

ISBN: 978-1-9822-0369-6 (sc)
ISBN: 978-1-9822-0371-9 (hc)
ISBN: 978-1-9822-0370-2 (e)

Library of Congress Control Number: 2018905402

Balboa Press rev. date: 05/29/2018

Psalm 23 (KJV)

The Lord is my shepherd; I shall not want.
He maketh me to lie down in green pastures: he leadeth me beside the still waters.
He restoreth my soul: he leadeth me in the paths of righteousness for his name's sake.
*Yea, though I walk through the valley of the shadow of death, I will fear no evil: **for thou art with me**; thy rod and thy staff they comfort me.*
Thou preparest a table before me in the presence of mine enemies: thou anointest my head with oil; my cup runneth over.
Surely goodness and mercy shall follow me all the days of my life: and I will dwell in the house of the Lord forever.

This book is dedicated to the glory of God,
in thanksgiving for my family, friends, and medical staff
who saw me safely through this journey.

CONTENTS

POSTLUDE

POSTSCRIPT

PREFACE

"When morning gilds the skies,
My heart, awaking cries:,
May Jesus Christ be praised!"
Anonymous German Hymn

I love the quiet in the early morning, before the dawn breaks. I silently slip out of bed, so as to not awaken my husband, grab my robe from the hook on the bathroom door, slide my feet into my waiting slippers, and glide through the darkened house without even attempting to turn on a light. I start the coffee, only by the light on the rising glow outside the kitchen windows, soaking in the peace of a new day.

This has always been "my time," and I do not want to share it with anyone right away. I don't wish for conversation or food or even a devotion book at first. For those first few minutes, I only yearn to hear the twitter of the birds in the yard, the whirr of the hummingbirds at the feeder, the crickets or cicadas sawing their raspy songs, the drip of the kitchen faucet and the coffeemaker, the hum of the refrigerator. All these voices of my morning, like an orchestra tuning up before a concert, create a cacophony of peace I can feel down to my toes. I am safe. I am alive. I am blessed.

When I was diagnosed with ovarian cancer, my life changed dramatically and instantly from one of creative effort and joy to inability and pain. So it was not surprising when, during the long nights with pain robbing me of sleep, I intuitively made my way through the darkened house once more to seek my "spot" on the little loveseat in the kitchen, armed with paper and pen, phone, or computer. When the words began to flow, almost faster than I was able to transcribe them onto the paper or screen, my sickness became the vessel from which my blessings flowed.

I found writing poetry a cathartic exercise for the pain, doubt, fear, and inactivity I was experiencing. Each poem I wrote began in pain, yet ended in praise—and none of it was contrived. The poetry served to help me work through the pain, simultaneously expressing thanks to God for all my blessings I had been given day to day. My focus shifted from my bodily aches to the rhythm of the words, comforting me, lulling me, as a mother rocking her child. How profoundly I knew God was right there beside me in the stillness of the night.

This compilation of my poems is a journey of my mind, denoting both the good and the bad of chemotherapy, ordered solitude, sleeplessness, and discomfort that comes from cancer. For a cancer patient, trying to stay positive and cheerful, even on rough days, is the hardest job of all; yet it is so important in the healing of the body and mind. In some of the poems, the words are laced with humor, bringing an incredible lightness to a dark subject, and consequently raising my spirits as I wrote. Since I could rarely use my stiffened and neuropathic hands for painting, drawing, or playing the violin as I once had done, I began to paint verbal pictures in verse to describe my days, inevitably creating a legacy of my year of recuperation.

This book could not have been created without the encouragement from those with whom I had shared some of the poems. Often I was asked permission to share a poem with other cancer patients, to offer comfort and assurance to them as well. Thus, this collection has been published with the hope that my time of cancer and treatment might help those in similar circumstances. I organized it in the order the poems were written, to show my progression through the illness from the time I felt my worst, to when I was gaining strength and hope.

There was never any question as to the title of my book. In each poem is the theme of God's continuing presence. While reading Psalm 23, the visual images of the comforting passages always come to mind—green pastures, still waters, overflowing cup of blessings—encircling the four words, *"For Thou art with me,"* in a framework of peace.

Of all the passages in the Bible, Psalm 23 is my favorite. Memorized long before I could read, it was written on my heart by my parents, who recited it often as we children were tucked in at night. When reading it, I am always amazed how every phrase holds special meaning to me, as the rhythm of the soft and comforting words permeate my soul. During my chemotherapy treatments, I would repeat this psalm over and over in my mind, as the drip of the IV filled my veins with both chaos and healing.

We never know which everyday events will shape our lives or give us avenues to help us find our peace. A half-century of couch time in a darkened room at dawn became my haven and altar during the times when, because of the pain of surgery and chemo, my heart was even darker. As I *"walked through the valley of the shadow of death,"* I, like the psalmist, felt God's comforting presence (Psalm 23); and, yes, *"My cup runneth over."* (Psalm 23, KJV)

AUGUST

In August 2016, as I made my way down to Louisiana to visit my grandchildren and daughter, I decided to detour by Lake Village Medical Clinic for a quick checkup, thinking I was having a bout with diverticulitis. During my checkup, however, Dr. Burge felt something suspicious and sent me to the local hospital for further testing. Discovering a mass, he immediately turned my face toward Houston for validation and treatment. My daughter Jody, a physician in Alexandria, Louisiana, arranged for a second opinion with an oncologist the next day. By the following week, I was heading to MD Anderson Cancer Center to meet with Dr. Pedro Ramirez, who, after confirming the diagnosis through further testing, scheduled surgery for removal of the large tumor. My life as I had known it had completely changed.

Diagnosis Day in Houston

For a cancer patient, the days between diagnosis and surgery are filled with unknown terrors one tries to suppress. In a fog of expectancy and dread, laced with both hope and denial, my husband and I stiffly moved through the preparations of packing and leaving our Arkansas home for an extended time; driving south to our daughter's home in Louisiana; and then, with her at the wheel, continuing five more hours to Houston's M D Anderson Cancer Center.

When I recall that time of shock, acceptance, and preparation, I am keenly aware of how gently we were sent on our journey by the "*goodness and mercy*" (Psalm 23 KJV) of our friends and neighbors offering to help. Essential things that had to be done prior to leaving were quickly and efficiently checked off the lengthy list.

Eight years prior, our daughter, Jody, had arrived at the cancer center by ambulance with her sick husband in the dark of the night, remaining there eight months for his chemotherapy treatments, bone marrow transplant, and subsequent recovery from leukemia. So it was that, years later, she served as our personal and knowledgeable guide into the vast network of hospitals at Texas Medical Center. Learning the protocol of such a system can be as stressful as the disease itself, and we were spared that sense of unease. God had truly prepared a place for us "*in the presence of mine enemies*" (Psalm 23 KJV).

Back home, during the long days before my surgery, a wise friend suggested that I should write an upbeat letter to distract not only my own fears of the upcoming surgery, but also that of my family and friends who could read it in the waiting room during the procedure. I decided to write a funny poem instead, hoping to lighten things up a bit. It backfired: They all bawled and squalled!

Surgical Prelude

I know what's going on out there,
While I am being cut,
Dissected to de-tumor me
From neck down to my gut.

("Muth-ther!", I hear my son cry,
At reading that last word,
But when you are twixt now and then,
A verbal freedom's heard.)

But I digress. Now back on track:
You're getting sad and fearful!!
That attitude's not helping me!
Stop, Patty, being tearful!!

Put down your smart phones for a while;
Communicate together.
Enjoy the banter and some jokes,
Just talk about the weather.

I want it light and loving,
Just keep it 'laxed and calm;
Be close to one another;
For each one's wounds, a balm.

Charles, I could use a prayer or two,
For heavenly protection,
May I suggest a small bequest
Concerning my dissection?

"I'd like to stick around, dear God,
For several years ahead;
So would You please consider
To make me healed instead?

I feel I have abilities
To help those whom I meet;
I'd like to think that I can be
Your earthly hands and feet.

My husband often asks me
To solve the mystery
Of where he laid his hearing aids,
(A daily history!)

Although my daughter's charting
A new course for her life,
I'd like to be a witness
That she will have less strife.

And, yes, there's my son, way up north,
Who can't stop by and chat;
I must be healed to visit him,
So help me, God, with that.

The grandkids need me, Father,
To tutor them in math,
To pay for LEGOs, bows, and things,
To stop the hints of sass.

So if it's not a bother,
Please leave me here awhile,
So I can cook and draw and play
And walk another mile."

Bob, this may be a good time
To show shots of your trip,
Comparing destinations,
Of new wines that you sipped.

And Patty, you and Charles can swap
Some ideas of design,
'Cause we all know that both your homes
Are looking mighty fine!

My husband might need company
To walk and move a bit
Up, down, and round the hallways--
It's hard for him to sit!

The next few days, in many ways,
May prove quite hard for you,
But it's essential to ensure
That I get all I'm due!

Yes, first I'll set some basic rules
For my recuperating;
It's ME, ME, ME you'll focus on!!!!!
(An idea I'm not hating!)

My First Rule: In recovery,
When you come back to see me,
Make sure, girls, that I look my best
All covered to my knees!

My hair could use some combing,
A little lip gloss, too;
Some lotion on my hands and feet,
(You missed a spot or two!)

And when I get into a room,
It will get even better:
These rules below delineate
My terms, down to the letter.

"Go fetch me this!" "Go get me that!"
I may be heard to bellow.
"Now go and do it double-time!"
(Thanks, Bart, that's a nice fellow!)

"Now fluff the pillow, change the bed,
Hand me a Coke on ice!"
(I have to say, even through the pain,
This all is very nice!)

I know I'll have to be weaned off
My megalomanic level;
But until then, I will enjoy
Just acting like a devil!

What's that you whispered, Son, to them?
"That seems just like before"?
(Now don't go there, or I will swear
To boot you out the door!)

Rule Number Two: Arrange my drains,
My tubes, my bags, my lines,
Creatively, and neatly, too:
I sure want to look FINE

When handsome doctors hear my heart,
When nurses check my vitals,
I'll lie in state, cooperate,
And add another title:

"There's Dr. Judith Bynum,
The Best of All Our Patients!
They come from near, they come from far,
They journey from all nations!"

They want to see recovery
Not like they've seen before!
I'll be in record books of hope
And get a super score!

(Who knows? They may make plaques of brass
Engraved with name and day.
They'll even name a wing for me
Right here at MDA!)

Let's move ahead to Number Three:
Take care of one another.
You'll have to fry the chicken, and
You'll have to play the mother.

It's you who'll write the little notes
To check on each of you.
I get to rest (I do that best!)--
There's still so much to do!

Although this little ditty
Was penned to lighten things,
It surely doesn't minimize
The love and peace you bring

In being here, while I am there,
In looking after Bart,
In sending up a prayer or two
That comes straight from your heart.

I want to keep it positive;
I want no wringing hands.
My faith still grows, and this it shows:
It's on my faith I stand.

I'm getting well, that much I'm sure,
It might just take a while,
But I can guarantee to you,
I'll go another mile!

SEPTEMBER

Thanks to the amnesic effect of anesthesia, the week of my surgery is mostly a blur. The first three days were difficult, although softened by medications. Although any movement at all brought raw, searing pain, I diligently walked the halls several times the day after surgery, following my doctor's orders to the limit. The sheer effort, however, left me exhausted with pain that simply would not abate, setting me back to immobility and extreme nausea for the next two days.

After I was discharged, we moved to a nearby hotel for several days before attempting to drive to my daughter's home, where we remained for another week. As soon as I began feeling stronger, however, we weathered the jolting, four-hour drive back to our little farm in Collins, Arkansas. It was so good to be home!

Although I had had several surgeries in my lifetime, never had I endured one that was accompanied by such uncertainty of the future. *"Did they get it all?"* was my constant thought. I was aware that I had many months ahead of me until I knew the answer; and in the interim, I needed a diversion. During one, long, uncomfortable night at the hotel, I had begun to mindlessly create a poem about three exaggerated characters who comically personified the nature of my pain. Through this creative process, I felt myself responding to the rhythm and mental exercise it offered, lifting my spirits. While I focused on writing the verses, thereby laughing at my pain, I realized it had not monopolized my every thought! God had given me a *"rod and staff"* to *"comfort me"* (Psalm 23 KJV) by channeling my thoughts, thereby relaxing both my body and mind!

The Chainsaw, the Glass, and the Razor Blades

The chainsaw, the glass, and the razor blades
Went out on the town one night.
Their new residence was in evidence
Where the tumor once hung tight.

Near my navel, the three got a table
And ordered a round of stiff drinks.
And before very long, the drinks became strong
And unloosed their worst nature of things.

The three lumbered o'er onto the dance floor,
Slicing and cutting their way.
As the music revived, the pain came alive
And created havoc all day!

Now thanks to the meds, the three blades are dead,
Although they have been known to revive
If coughing occurs, or bending berserk
Causes dancing pains to come alive!

The moral herein you can take with a grin
To hopefully laugh at the pain,
Giving power to my goal of taking the role
To conquer again and again.

Humor may be a tool, they say, of the fool,
But it's easy to keep near at hand.
So I'll laugh at you, Pain, not allow you to gain
When the cough once more strikes up the band. Amen!

A Day at a Time

"Just take it a day at a time," others say;
"Just live in the moment--no more."
It's easy to nod in agreement
When not knowing what Life has in store.

"You're brave, you're courageous, you're strong," doctors brag.
"You're our number one patient," they spake;
Then the numbness subsides, and the pain springs alive,
And I know that I'm truly a fake.

For all of my life, I saw others,
When going through cancer and pain,
Their faith would start lagging, their spirits were dragging--
Yet their faith resurrected again.

And I thought that, "Oh yes, I can do this!
I'm ready to go through the pain!"
Then the truth showed its face in a very short space
When discomfort arose and remained.

I've read in the Bible how Jesus
Suffered for us, and God did allow;
But the true definition of suffering's attrition
I'd not understood until now.

How pain wraps its sharp claws so tightly,
How it grips by its razor-sharp teeth.
The breaths become ragged, the body grows haggard,
Free-falling with nothing beneath.

That's the time that I see my true mettle;
That's the part of my life when I learn
The comfort God sends, the quiet He lends;
His True Love for me now I discern.

"Be still!" God commands, and I listen.
"Breath and pause!" and my body obeys.
My pain is surrendered; true peace is engendered
As I face yet another long day.

And what shall I learn from this era?
What's the reason for enduring such pain?
I'd guess, at my best, my Faith's put to test,
And new closeness to God is my gain.

I know prayers sent from others bring solace;
I feel grateful in wake of kind deeds.
And when all viewed together, I am sure I can weather,
With my Heavenly Father, my needs.

So thank you, dear God, for your nearness
On this path through the forest of night.
And I pray that someday, I'll emerge from the fray
To continue my journey toward Light.

OCTOBER

By now, my patience was wearing thin, as was I. Eating was out of the question, and most days I was only able to swallow a few bites of soup or dry toast. My weight dropped several pounds each week, until finally the scales showed a loss of almost forty pounds.

During my initial chemotherapy, I suffered a violent reaction to one of the chemos. Immediately, the nurse added large doses of steroids and Benedryl to the IV for several hours, then slowed the chemo drip from four hours to ten. Although the time seemed arduous for me, I realized how awful it must have been for my daughter and husband, sitting quietly beside my bed all that time. The hands on the wall clock crawled minute-by-minute, hour-by-hour. I was miserable from the high dose of steroids, with its side effects of overwhelming frustration and depression. For my family, I was not a nice person. For the first time, I understood well the biblical story of the pigs running off the edge of the cliff!

Within a few hours after the return flight back to Arkansas, I began running a fever; so I was instructed by MDA to go immediately to the nearest ER. For three days, I was hospitalized, until I was strong enough to be flown back to Houston. My children met us at the ER there, where tests were immediately run. After my surgery to remove a large abdominal abscess, my son took the night shift at my bedside, allowing his exhausted sister to crash for a much-needed rest at the hotel. My brother also flew in, to be with my husband, and a close friend meet us back in Arkansas to help out for another few days. The reality of how ill I really was had become crystal clear.

Sibling Support after Surgery

Cancer and chemo change everything! After I lost my hair, it became hard for me to try to look my best. The initial hair loss was more of an emotional shock than I had expected it to be, so I searched for ways to soften the blow of the mirror's image. I tried tying scarves, test-driving wigs, or purchasing hats and knit caps to hide my baldness, with little success. Until one day, I found my comfort zone was to simply "let it be!"

By this time, my prayers had become an intimate, unending flow of conversation with God, and every little nuance of kindness shown filled and thrilled me with both tears and newfound joy. As the chemo simultaneously wreaked both its havoc and its cure, I began thinking more and more about those whom I had loved and lost, such as my parents and sister who had been gone for decades. How blessed I had been all my life, both as a child and as an adult, surrounded by such wonderful people!

Very few people are given a year to drop out of life, a period of time and grace to think deeply and profoundly about what they truly believe. With its wrapper a bit torn around the edges and the ribbon frayed, cancer gave me this gift.

The Impatient Patient

Why do they call me a patient
When I am so obviously not?
I want to do things as I used to,
But not with the problems I've got!

My caregivers question my motives
On each little move that I take.
They offer bland food, a little prunes stewed,
And more broth than I want, goodness sake!

Each day I awaken so hopeful—
Will it be the one where I say,
"My pain's gone away! Hip, Hip, and Hurray!"?
But so far, the answer is, "Nay."

Eight glasses of water? Good golly!
Eight walks down the hall, Heavens no!
Eight meals every day full of protein?
If I do it, the pain's apt to go?

Healing time is just not Central Standard
Or Mountain, Pacific, or East;
Instead, it's God's Time that makes people fine
When their will to control is released.

So maybe one day I'll be patient,
In every sense of the word.
Throw my Timex away, send up praises all day,
To my Heavenly Father and Lord.

Changes

My mama always told me
To try to look so neat,
With hair all washed, with dresses ironed,
Shined shoes upon my feet.

For nearly seven decades,
I've made my mama proud;
Then cancer came into my life
And shouted very loud:

"I'm here to rearrange your life!
I'm here to change your stance!
I'll snuff out all your vanity,
If I have half a chance!

"I'll leave you scarred, I'll leave you bald,
I'll make you hurt all over!
I'll make you toss your makeup
And leave scarves in the drawer!

"Your appetite will not remain,
Nor will your strength and humor"—
(Now who'd have thought that all of this
Could be caused by a tumor??")

So now the battle line is drawn;
I must make a decision:
I face my foe, let cancer know
I view it with derision.

The power it wields can be contained;
But changes it bestows
Can be attained, my courage drained—
If I allow it so.

I draw my sword of warfare;
I call in all the troops.
And with a mighty surge of Faith,
I yell a loud war whoop!

For God is by my side, you know,
He raises high his staff—
The winds erase the sandy line
That barricades the path.

The angels in their chariots fly,
Lined shoulder next to shoulder;
While Christian soldiers with their spears
March onward, ever bolder.

His staff he drops, the winds subside,
He gathers me to Him.
He calms my fears and dries my tears
And makes me smile again.

My baldness is a sign, you see,
That I am still alive!
So I will wear it proudly
While here on earth, I'll strive

To praise my God forevermore
More glory to His name,
Allowing me to honor Him,
To further spread His fame.

When once again I'll brush my hair
Or shine my shoes and such,
I'll never be the same again—
These things won't matter much.

New clothes lost their importance;
My smile is all I need!
I'm simply free to be just me,
To plant more Christian seeds.

So long as I have peace and love,
So long His honor give,
I'll be His best, I'll pass the test,
To praise Him while I live.

Retrospection

I think I have my daddy's hands,
His eyes and blonde hair, too,
Although, as years are adding on,
My eyes seem paler blue.

My silky hair, now turning white,
Reminds me more and more
Of his Brylcremed crown that bleached out
When he was twenty-four.

I think I have my mother's smile,
Her artsy side, her drive,
Although these days I hardly have
Enough zip to survive!

It seems I sorely miss them more
While I am fighting pain;
I wish to have a day with them,
A time near them again.

My sister's right beside them
A-sitting on the clouds;
I hope she knows I always boast:
Her courage made me proud!

Her cancer lasted three long years,
Yet never did she falter.
I wonder if I did enough
To help her like I ought to.

I have a million questions
Of chemo, sickness, pain.
She tried so hard to press on toward
A healthy life again.

But now they're on the other side.
They're hale and happy, too.
Eternally they wait for me
And for my brother, too.

But I'm not ready for the bar!
I'd like to wait some more!
I want to see my grandkids grow,
See what Life has in store.

I want to help my husband
And both my children, too;
I feel I need a few more years,
Cause I have work to do!

Please, God, allow my sickly frame
To once again get well.
Just give my folks a message that
More years on earth I'll dwell.

But someday soon, I'll join them
Behind the Pearly Gates
For one great big reunion, but
Not yet, for heaven's sake!

Insignificance

If the whole world's in His hands,
Is there room enough for me?
The wars, the poverty, the hunger, the hate
Seem way too much, you see.

His eye is on the sparrow?
His arms surrounding me?
But I'm such a little, tiny speck
Of all humanity.

His wisdom is eternal,
I always have His ear.
The fact is that, above all else,
My God is always near.

This week I face an upward path
That's filled with rocks and rills;
But by His side, with Him my guide,
The climb will be fulfilled.

He does not promise smooth roads;
He does not promise ease;
But rather, He's a beacon
To light my way with peace.

So, yes, I know the truth is that
There's love enough for me,
As well as tiny little birds
From sea to shining sea.

I thank you, God, for being near.
I thank You for my care.
I praise and glorify You
Always and everywhere.

NOVEMBER

My second chemo treatment hit a bump—another bad reaction. Initially I had been prescribed two chemos, but my body was continuing to refuse one of them. Although my doctor tried to assure me, I began losing hope that I might be cured. I didn't feel like eating, and my weight continued to drop. This was a critical time.

The solitude of a quiet and peaceful home in the country was perfect for recuperation. Because of my low blood count and accompanying weakness, I was completely homebound, not allowed to go anywhere near crowds or germs. Life slowed, and I begin to grasp the concept that I no longer should look into the future. As a dear friend reminded me daily, "Live in the moment, one day at a time, and, sometimes, even one hour at a time!" She added, "And give thanks to God for each of these precious moments." Every hour was a gift, a time for the chemo to do its job, no matter how arduous the process seemed to be, and a time to simply be alive.

As the weeks passed slowly, I became increasingly aware God, not I, was in charge of my life. I had to trust Him completely, not partially. This simple but powerful statement finally arose to the conscious level, forcing me to accept the fact that I was only a passenger on this ride of Life, not the engineer! For the "Coordinator of All Events", as my family had always called me, this was a big step forward on my spiritual journey, as well as my physical one.

As Thanksgiving approached, my daughter announced that she and her family were coming to the farm, where she would cook the feast. We were making it simple, without frills, however. My husband bought the essential groceries needed for the pared-down menu, complete with paper plates. On Thanksgiving morning, our friend Faye called to say she was going to send "a casserole or two" before noon to complete our meal. When her husband and daughter knocked on our door, their arms were laden with homemade casseroles, breads, and a variety of desserts! The Pilgrims never had it so good! Once more, God had provided.

Chemo Companion

God came with me to the clinic,
Walked beside me, held my hand;
Calmed my heart and stilled my being,
Helped me when I had to stand.

God is present, right beside me,
Inside both my head and heart,
Adding Peace into the IV,
Adding Love when chemo starts.

With the liquid slowly dripping,
While my silent prayers are said,
I will faithfully surrender
To my God, upon my bed.

With Him, I shall change my thinking
From a dread, to gratitude
For the chemo that's encircling
Round the tumor's magnitude.

Viewing it more as a blessing
Than a time of poison pain,
I will visualize the healing,
Hoping to get well again.

Now as I lay on the gurney,
Praying for a sweet release
Of the cancer's spell that binds me,
That the clutching pain will cease,

I'll remember He's my Maker,
He's my Comfort, He's my Guide;
With my Heavenly Father's presence,
I'll have healing bonafide.

God went with me to the clinic,
As He does where'er I go;
He will never, ever leave me--
My God, from whom all blessings flow!

One More Day, Lord

One more day, Lord.
That's all I can hope.
One more day, Lord,
Is all I can cope.

Life is hard now
With its aches and pains.
One more day, Lord,
Is all I can gain.

Cancer struck me,
And surgery done;
I had chemo
With reactions full run.

Sickness followed,
With days of no fun.
Don't see my future
Down under the sun.

One more day, Lord,
To maybe feel well.
One more day, Lord,
To hopefully tell

That I'm healing
And soon be on task.
One more day, Lord,
Is all that I ask.

Thank you, Father,
For prayers from my friends;
Thank you, Jesus,
For family who tends

To my health needs
And bolsters my faith.
One more day, Lord,
Is my only way.

DECEMBER

I have always loved December, with the flurry of planning, decorating, and shopping for perfect gifts for family and friends. This year, however, I did my shopping by phone and online from the armchair, since I had been quarantined from public shopping areas.

With the holidays upon me, my energy level had plummeted too low to even send Christmas cards, as I had done for almost a half-century. Decorations had to be minimal, since weakness would not allow me to participate or even to direct my husband in unpacking and displaying ornaments. Accepting the fact that a decorated tree would be nigh impossible, I chose my sole holiday décor to be the beautiful nativity scene painted by my sister years earlier. Through it, Jesus' birth was in the forefront of our thoughts during Christmas, as never before.

Each year, our holiday season traditionally begins with a trip to Albany, New York, to hear Handel's *Messiah* conducted by our son Woody, the music director of a large cathedral. This year, however, it was not to be. Not only would we miss hearing the beautiful concert, but also it would be the first time our son had conducted it without our being present. On the evening of the concert, our neighbor, Charles, who was visiting in Connecticut, drove to Albany to represent us there as "family." What an humbling Christmas gift beyond measure!

Overall, our Christmas turned out to be one of the best, even without my usual baking, cleaning, wrapping, coordinating, and travelling north. I even felt well enough for us to make the trip to Alexandria for Christmas Day with the grandchildren. That year, I learned to keep it simple, slow down, focus solely on Christmas as the birthday of Christ, and to just be deeply grateful for Life itself. Without my usual exhausting physical involvement, Christmas became even more Christ-centered, meaningful, and peaceful for us.

Coping at Christmas

I'm all out of steam, Lord,
My energy's spent.
Don't know what soul took it,
Or whither it went.

I just know it left me
Some time before dawn,
Between last night's sleeping
And morning's first yawn.

My laughter went with it
And left me quite down;
I can't get excited
To go into town!

With Christmas upon us
And gifts to be bought,
A good shopping spree
Was well needed, I thought.

But the mind is not always
In control of the will.
Just the thought of the chill
In the air keeps me still.

I can't rise above
The discomforting cold,
When I step out the doorway,
Trying hard to be bold.

I used to be hardy—
But now look at me!
I'm a coward to Cold;
That's quite awful to see!

It's not really the weather,
If I'm honest with you—
My stamina's lacking,
As it tends to do.

I don't like to admit it,
But I'm not at all well,
And when I'll get better,
Only more time will tell.

Maybe a trip
Into town is one way
To raise up my spirits
Much higher today.

Enjoying the excitement
That shopping allows
May at least offer respite
From sitting for hours.

Will it be wiser
At helping me weather
The storms of the chemo,
And make me feel better?

Or should I surrender
To minding the things
That my medical team
In their wise counsel brings?

My God, make me stronger
To not yield in haste
To temptations that flash
Right in front of my face!

The storefronts so pretty,
Filled with Christmas delights
Are drawing me in
On this cold, winter night..

I think I hear catalogs
Calling to me
To pick them up, order,
Then wait patiently.

My order's delivered
Right up to my door,
And I don't have to endure
Biting cold anymore!

I've finished my shopping,
My credit card's maxed.
Now all I must do is
Sit back and relax!

JANUARY

After each treatment, the chemotherapy continued to leave me unbelievably weak. On treatment days, we usually were unable to leave the hospital until late in the evening, exhausted both emotionally and physically. I needed to eat a bite, but the sheer thought of food was nauseating. Many times, a smoothie from a drive-through or a clear soup from a deli was our supper. Although literally staggering from their weariness, my husband and daughter always tried to make me as comfortable as possible before turning off the light.

Heavy with steroids, rife with chemo, hardly able to talk or walk from sheer fatigue, I just wanted to curl up in bed and fall asleep to erase the stress of the day. Many times, I was unable to relax, however, because of the battle waging internally between the heavy load of steroids coursing through my veins, (making me jittery and wide awake), and the chemo I had taken, (causing weakness and fatigue). In addition, the neuropathy made the sheer touch of the sheet very uncomfortable.

Some time during the night, I usually moved into the living room of the hotel suite, so that my insomnia did not compromise my family's rest. Lying on the loveseat, I folded my long legs up under me while snuggling down into the fleecy warmth of an afghan. I welcomed the dark solitude, where it was just God and me. During these long, sleepless nights, I was the most vulnerable, yet strangely the most comfortable spiritually. I could honestly open my heart to my Father in long hours of deep prayer. God was right beside me, and He comforted me through the night.

During the days of treatment and subsequent days and nights of gaining strength, I was aware that many people were praying for me, just as I had done for others as well during my life. What I had not realized until the offered prayers were specifically for me, however, was that I could physically feel the intercessory prayers, like a weighted blanket of security draped around my shoulders.

As I faced another birthday, I wanted it to be a time of gratitude, both for my life and for those who had been so attentive and helpful during my illness. Writing a poem of thanks, I texted it to friends whose kindnesses had made all the difference in the past few months. For me, it was truly a gift from the heart.

Chemo Time is Here

Back to my couch,
I die a little bit;
Bad cells, some good,
They cry a little bit.
Poisoning and cleaning,
To fry a little bit—
Chemo time is here.

Good days turn bad,
In just a few short hours;
Food that I eat now
Turns bitter, bland, and sour.
Pendulum swings downward
Changing personality to dour—
Chemo time is here.

It seems I'd remember
The havoc it wreaks!
It's been since September
The purpose it seeks,
Leaving pain in its wake
Leaving body so weak—
It's chemo time again.

That's when I must recognize
The negativity that's straining
To break through the walls
Of my faith and Christian training;
I reach for God's strong hand,
My heart and soul's demanding—
Comfort time is here.

There's never a time
When I reach out, that He's not there.
I may move away from Him,
But He calls me back with care.
His nearness fills my heart,
Bringing peace and love to share—
Yes, comfort time is here.

It's a time for "being still,"
To listen well and know;
It's a space for softly healing
My body and spirit both.
It's a blessing of quiet days
To actively show—
My God is always here!

My Sixty-Ninth

That's right, today I'm sixty-nine;
Um-hmm, oh yeah, 'tis true.
While I used to quake at seventy,
Now it's not so bad a view!

Though cancer is my enemy,
It's taught me quite a lot,
Including how each hour, each day
Is such a gift from God.

I fill my time with positives,
Like books to soothe my spirit,
Or a woodland walk or a friendly talk
To anyone who'll hear it.

Another lesson cancer shows—
To practice "being still."
I must turn off the brain-sounds
To know my Master's will.

That still, small voice is hard to hear
O'er heady conversations
Between the Present and What-Ifs
In my brain thinking station!

With all that roar, how can the door
Be open for God's whisper?
It's like, as teens so long ago,
I couldn't hear my sister!

When chemo's running through my veins,
Attacking all it meets,
The room is dark and still and quiet—
And God a vigil keeps.

I hear His voice, I feel His touch,
With family so near;
They quietly sit so patiently
And whisper in my ear.

I've learned to recognize the worth
Of every little thing—
Like comfort from a caring smile,
My morning cup to drink.

Such is the pleasure it affords
When friends take time to text,
Or call or send a get-well card:
(I wonder what is next!)

No matter what the others think
As in their days, they hurry;
I watch the songbirds feed for hours
Or squirrels as they scurry.

It's nice to have this peaceful time
To concentrate on things
Like legacies and lessons
My pondering will bring.

So thank you, God, for little things,
For blessings barely seen;
I'm glad I've had this time to sit
And think what these things mean.

Although there's been the pain and such,
It's time for reconnection;
A time to sift through keepsakes;
A time of true reflection.

So as I greet my sixty-ninth,
I well consider all
The many blessings of my life,
Both big and very small.

Just know that, friends, while reading this,
You're in the numbered list.
I thank my God for all you are
To me, and all you've been.

My life was carefully carved by God:
He gave my thoughts a map;
The torch He gave was always lit
To guide when lost, perhaps.

So as I march toward seventy,
Know well that He's the plan
Of who I am and what I am:
I thank you, Lord. Amen!

FEBRUARY

Somehow it never occurred to me that I might have cancer during my lifetime. The single incidence of cancer on either side of my family was my sister, Mary, who, at fifty-four, died of breast cancer twenty years ago. Instead, our family was rife with heart attacks, strokes, and lots of deaths from old age and natural causes! So it was that I entered into a totally unfamiliar world of cancer treatments, side effects, and subsequent physical changes.

As only a cancer patient truly understands, the fatigue that follows treatments sometimes takes on a life of its own. The term "bone-weary" comes to mind when trying to describe it. Moving from one room to another, even from one chair to another, left me breathless and huffing. My mind was still on overdrive with things I wanted to do, while my still-weakened body remained in neutral or reverse. After straining for weeks to get in and out of bed, I finally succumbed to the repeated suggestion to install a bedrail. Wow...I had hit old age, I thought. After a night of once again having the leverage to stand more easily, though, I was ashamed that pride had kept me from ordering it sooner.

As I progressed through the chemotherapy, there were times when it became increasingly difficult to keep my spirits up. I dreaded upcoming treatments, afraid I would have another bad reaction. After a third and more severe one, my doctor finally made the decision to stop it, for fear of permanently damaging one of my organs in the process. It was both a relief and a concern: *Was getting only one chemo going to change my prognosis?*

Life was marching forward and moving on, but I was not moving with it. I continued my nightly vigils with prayer, devotional books, earmarked Bible, and pen and paper nearby, still getting comfort from them all. Over time, however, doubt crept in, dragging my faith down in the process. On most days, I still managed to wear a mask of positivity on the outside, even though, down in my spirit, I felt bereft. I had arrived at the place where I had to prove my complete faith in God, that I could give it all to Him, and that I could face each day with prayer-filled determination. With Him, I could get through this! These were not mere words: It was the pivotal point in my spiritual life.

Weary but Blessed

I'm very tired, Lord,
Of cancelling flights,
Of postponing appointments,
Of sitting up nights.

I'm so weary, God,
Of aches, pains--and pills
That try to erase them,
But just make me ill.

I'm, oh, so upset, Lord,
That no balance exists
In the good and the bad--
That's one thing that I miss.

Since Life took a turn
While age took its toll,
Both husband and I
Seem to be on a roll.

The cancer is over,
But not all the pain.
I don't know that I'll
Ever fiddle again.

Then vertigo stuck--
Add that to the mix.
I list to the right--
What a terrible fix!

So where did my zip go?
My energy's spent!
I've searched for it daily:
Don't know where it went!

Just sitting and sleeping
And watching the telly
Fills much of my days,
Besides feeding my belly.

No small talk we share?
A thing of the past.
It's big talk we need now
While our hearing still lasts!

I realize that I
Should not ever complain;
But, gee, Lord, my hymns
Sound much more like refrains.

Oh, please, will you send me
A respite it two?
I'm due for a break--
I have so much to do!

I know there are others
Much worse off than me.
But, darn it, it's my turn
To once more be free!

But wait--did I lose track
Of all of my blessings?
(I've been so shortsighted,
I now am confessing.)

God's still, little voice
Has been drowned out by woe--
So I must stop complaining!
This much I know.

My pity time's over--
Five minutes allowed!
My praise time's beginning,
With prayers said out loud!

Thank you, dear Father,
For all of my blessings,
For friends who support me
When I need some lessons

On staying quite still,
On living today,
On treasuring Life
In every way.

For I have been blessed
Every day that I've lived,
And I feel I need more time
To give what I give.

I praise you, dear Father,
From whom blessings flow,
Please stay close beside me
Wherever I go.

Please bless those around me,
As well as those far--
And help me remember
How special they are.

But most of all, Father,
Please forgive when I falter,
Or don't keep my eyes, brain,
And heart on Your altar.

I know I'm not perfect;
I have lots to change,
So I'll keep on trying,
And all in Your Name.

Valentine's Day

It's Valentine's Day! A time for Love
To rain on earth from heaven above;
To pause from Life to share a minute,
To tell my friends how they are in it.

I've gone through minutes, hours, and days,
Sometimes not honoring the ways
That those around me helped me cope
And, consequently, gave new hope.

I've had some times I needed prayer
Offered up from here and there
For soothing aches, for staunching pain,
In hopes I might feel good again.

Yes, prayers are gifts from those like you
Who took the time and followed through;
You asked dear God to comfort me,
And I accepted thankfully.

Prayer works! I feel it as it's said,
From pinky toe to top of head—
Like current surging through my brain,
And I am left at peace again.

So on this Holiday of Love,
I want to thank my God above
For those of you who've steadied me,
While down the chemo path I see

A tiny light, an eerie glow
Way in the distance as I go
Through the discomfort of the cure;
It magnifies my being sure

I will get well! I will be free!
A prelude for eternity!
My wings will wait for later date:
Now's not my Time, it's not my Fate.

And when God draws me home at last,
I'll glance behind, look at my past,
Then, facing God who offers grace,
Walk boldly toward Him, face-to-face.

It's not my call on when I'll go.
That's for my Father God to know;
So I will simply try to be
His vessel of humanity,

While living out the days I'm given.
It's a good life that I've been living.
I will continue on, with prayer,
To shower His love everywhere.

That's why I've stopped here on my way
To thank God on this special day,
To bask in sunshine, play in rain,
Until I go back Home again.

You friends have been His hands and feet
By ministering to those whom you meet:
And I appreciate your choosing me
To be among those that you seek.

You've offered valentines all year!
You've shown your love--and don't you fear
It's gone unnoticed--that I know,
Because I truly love you so!

You didn't need a stamp, you see,
To send your message capably.
I well received it hand-to-hand
When casseroles and texts you sent.

St. Valentine would be impressed
If he could see what you do best
Is showing others that you care
And spreading His love everywhere.

MARCH

As the time drew nearer for the PET scan that would determine if the surgery and chemo had done its job, I was petrified. All my self-assurance dissolved, as I waited alone in the little room for the scan to begin. Would the single chemo manage to do the job of the intended two? Had I done all I could to be healthier during the months of treatment? I had been careful to continue my wellness checks, such as my yearly mammogram and flu shot. But had I done enough?

When the results came back, I was stunned at first, then overjoyed. I couldn't believe it: I was cured! Driving back to Alexandria, we stopped for a celebratory steak dinner, and then, exiting off the interstate, detoured south for a walk on the beach at dusk. For the first time, I was returning from Houston without being too weak and ill from a treatment to stand, which in itself was a joy!

Cancer-free with Dr. Ramirez, my surgeon

We excitedly drove to our Arkansas home, ready for life to settle back to normal. Assuming I would immediately begin to feel better, however, I was not prepared for the aftershock of the side effects that were growing stronger. Many nights, the neuropathy in my hands and feet was so bad that I would sit up for hours, only to return to the bed at dawn. Osteoarthritis swelled my knuckles, and, for the first time in our marriage, I put away my wedding rings. Over the next few months, I began to understand that I must accept my new body as is, without wishing for the old. I might never be the same–but I was alive!

Through it all, God had walked with me--from the first day of treatment on the sidewalk outside the cancer center, to the day I was pronounced cured. On the sandy beach at the ocean's edge, looking out on the vast expanse of the sea, I was reminded that whatever happened next was all a part of His plan for me. I was still a work in progress, even in my altered state. And with that blessed assurance, I felt my faith grow stronger every day.

Celebrating at the seashore

Gratitude

I thank my God this morning
For the comfort He bestows,
From the sparse hair on my balding head
To way down to my toes;

From the brittle nails that chemo brings,
For the scar that splits my torso:
These just serve as my reminders
To make me grateful more so.

For my new-grown crop of Daddy's hair
That sits upon my head.
Why, it's been so easy not to style
When I get out of bed!

For my aches of muscle, pain of bone,
The creaks and groans to walk.
Why, what a conversation
If these body parts could talk!

I guess all these little blessings
Will remind me of His healing,
Since He's the one who led my way
To newfound health and feeling.

With my God as my Comforter,
And my friends helping, too,
I'll make the day in a better way
And boldly see it through!

Cancer-Free?

Cancer-free?
How can that be?
The chemo took
My death from me!

God said, "Not yet!"
I'm going to let
You have more years--
Go buy a pet!"

It's quite surreal
How now I feel--
Relief unbounded
That I'm healed!

Was it a dream?
That's what it seems:
An introspective
State of being.

The scars that healed
Show that it's real.
The stone has rolled,
New life revealed.

But take a look--
I'll have to cook
And clean my house,
Not read a book!

My husband will
No longer still
Be serving me,
My cup to fill--

Gee, thanks, Chemo!
Just "way to go!"
Have to say "yes"
Instead of "no"?

I'll soon rejoin
Life's pathway going,
Instead of others
Doing the doing.

I will not face
Life's hectic race,
But instead choose
What's best to face.

I'll be selective,
More reflective
On what's important
And what's rejected.

I've learned to stay
Quite still and pray,
Enjoy the ride
Of each new day.

Joy in the morn,
At new day's dawn.
Thanks be to God!
I've been reborn!!

Ode to the Mammogram

Mammogram morning—
Oh, what a warning!
I know it's essential;
The data's sequential.

But, Lord, what a pain!
Dread to do it again.
Gonna get squished
Just flat as a dish!

I've always been told
That as you get old,
You must have this test
For checking your breasts.

But as I recall,
There's no females involved
In inventing devices
Of imaging slices!

There's no doubt about it:
Though I have to allow it,
I'll not stop complaining
While in process I'm straining!

And, oh, what contortions
When bodily portions
Will be squeezed up and in it,
If just for a minute.

"Hold your breath," I'll be told,
As I'm about to explode,
Leaning in to the beast
As I'm pancaked beneath!

What the tech will not get
Is I won't have breathed yet,
And still not for a minute
While my breast is trapped in it!

Oh, now I digress—
Although causing great stress,
It's a true gift from God
(Though the wrapping's quite odd.)

We gals must endure
To prove nothing's truer
That women are stronger:
It is we who live longer.

This year, there's a way
To keep my pain at bay--
Got my test while still numb
From the surgery done!

"Does that hurt?" The tech asked,
As she worked at her task.
I replied, "Not at all!
I'm just having a ball!"

I kept smiling throughout it,
Never thought much about it,
Cause my nerve ends were healing
With no pain revealing!

But when next year gets here,
I'll be dragged by the ear
To return once again
To see what I'll withstand.

And while waiting my session,
I'll be counting my blessings
For the gift of this way
To survive one more day!

Midnight Musings

When I was told I'm cancer-free
It never once occurred to me
That I'd experience such flares
Of feeling like my muscles tear.

My body aches just everywhere,
It starts right here, it goes to there.
My nights are fitful, long and sweaty,
As if I'm stabbed with a machete!

And if I bend to pick up things,
I might as well be using wings,
'Cause every joint refuses all
When asked to help me vertical.

In all the time I took the chemo,
I don't recall being in such limbo
From bands of pain across my chest
And aching deep within my breasts.

My legs don't work right as they should,
Instead, they feel they're mired in mud.
I walk as if I'm wearing waders,
Adjusting arrival times to later.

My doctor asks repeatedly,
"Have you fallen or do you need
Support to get up out of bed?"
I answer, "No," and shake my head.

His question always puzzled me,
But now I understand, you see,
That he knew I'd be hurting more.
I didn't know what was in store.

I've tried to recommence my life
And not let others know the strife
Of nights and days of feeling bad,
Or inabilities I've had.

But more and more, I clearly see
What lies ahead, is that I be
Much less involved than I was before,
Accepting what Life has in store.

Sometimes, in hours of deep despair,
I must confess the faith I wear
Gets rather worn and not as strong—
I pray for relief all night long.

My fears arise, as long ago,
And I'm consumed by vertigo
Of feeling God has moved away
And left me all alone that day.

But I know better--He's right here!
I only need to voice my fears,
And He will make them go away,
Restoring hope, while prayers I say.

No, he's not moved: I did the walking.
Yes, I'm the one who ceased our talking.
My faith returns to keep me strong
To face the hurting all night long.

I do not know what lies ahead;
If I feel bad, I'll stay abed.
And when I wake at dawn with pain,
I'll just switch off the light again.

The rhythm of the ebb and flow—
The pain will come, the pain will go,
Soon registers down inside my brain
Just like an old and sweet refrain.

Yes, I'll endure the unknown verse
And look toward the coming chorus,
Assured that pain will come again
Tho maybe less, as time I gain.

"Praise God from whom all blessings flow,"
I sing out loud, I hum down low.
My body's feeling much less pain—
I think I'll go to sleep again!

APRIL

When my baldness began sprouting growth, I was anxious to know how the new hair would look. Obviously, from the beginning, it had a mind of its own. On the crown of my head were punky spikes of tuft, with a hint of wave and fuzz on the periphery. I was going to have curls! God had given me a permanent perm!

Unsure if I should cover my head or just show my baldness, I usually wrapped a scarf around it when going out in public. At home, I preferred leaving my head bare. I finally decided to keep it short in a boy cut, instead of letting it grow. It was hard, when people I knew walked right by, not recognizing the "old bald lady."

Feeling confident that I was well enough for an annual women's retreat in another state, I went...and ended up too sick to drive home. Although I had been concerned about the upcoming three-hour drive and my lagging stamina, I was bound and determined to go. This event had been my goal all during my illness, and I wasn't going to miss it! There was no room in my blind determination for any common sense. Pacing myself, stopping often, and drinking lots of water, I arrived in time to get a quick nap before others arrived. So far, so good.

The weekend was wonderful! I managed to rest often, yet attend all the discussions and meals. Until Sunday morning, that is. Rising before dawn to go downstairs and make the coffee, vertigo struck, forcing me to my knees. Since I had never experienced dizziness like that before, I was not expecting the room to swim with each and every turn of my head or movement of my eyes. Slowly I managed to blindly crawl back upstairs, with eyes closed and nausea rising. As I hit the door of our bathroom, my daughter, realizing something was very wrong, helped me into bed and administered some nausea meds.

For the next few hours, I lay motionless. I was totally helpless. "Be Still" became my mantra; and for the first time in my life, I truly understood its significance: When you are unable to move at all, God has your complete attention. Prayerfully, I accepted that I would have to miss the closing worship service. Lying quietly, a poem of goodbye began playing in my mind. As the nausea settled a little, I quickly jotted down the rhyme, hoping someone would read it to the group downstairs for me. A few minutes before they were to begin, the nausea miraculously abated; and I was able, with help, to make my way downstairs. There, as I lay on the couch, surrounded by this circle of friends, we worshipped together.

Since I was unable to drive myself back home, Jody met my husband and brother halfway. On the final part of the journey home, the sky turned dark, as we unknowingly headed directly into a tornado. Our relief was palpable when we finally turned into the driveway. I had paid dearly for my weekend apart, and I knew without a doubt, I was still a long, long way from being whole.

I've Got Curls!

All my life my hair's been straight--
Straight and fine and thin.
Childhood barrettes slid on down
When Momma put them in.

But chemo's changed its nature;
Its texture now is curls!
Can't wait to see it six months out
When all will be unfurled.

We've always known the Bible says
That good can come from bad,
And this is an example,
From the sickness that I had.

As kids, we straight-haired sisters
Had perms to force a curl;
But they looked more like lightning hit
And set our locks a-twirl!!

But finally after all these years,
God blessed me with a crown
Of curls and tiny little waves
Among my fluffy down.

And if that's not a "good from bad,"
I don't know what it means.
It's my reward for "being still"
And getting well, it seems.

So thank you, Lord, for permanently
Leaving a reminder
To all who view my newborn curls,
That this is so much kinder

Than growing back my same gray hair
That all fell out last fall.
Why, Shirley Temple would be green
If she could see it all!

I do realize that chemo hair
Does not always remain,
So probably I'll wake up soon
And see straight hair again.

But till that time, I'll fluff my curls,
I'll brush my locks, and preen;
And just enjoy God's gift to me--
While it can still be seen!

Q-tips!

I looked in the mirror,
And what did I see?
A tall, white-topped Q-tip
Was looking at me!

The head on the body
Was "right out of the box,"
All covered with white down,
Instead of grey locks.

The stem of the Q-tip,
However, was bent;
(A refund from Johnson's
Might need to be sent!)

For, right down the middle
There was a red seam.
And it wasn't too straight,
If you know what I mean.

The neck of the cotton
Was rather well-creased,
And the rest was all rippled
Down to where the stem ceased.

But wait! There's another
Snow-white Q-tip that's squatty,
Built like a rolled bandage
All down its stem body.

Not blessed with a neck,
Head has no protrusion--
A long, iced-topped cake
Is its first-sight illusion!

We Q-tips will maybe
Make other folks gawk
When they're passing us by
On the city sidewalks.

But please be assured,
Although with imperfection,
We will hold our heads high
As we head our direction.

From the end of our sticks
To the top of our swabs,
We're the softest and finest,
Created by God!

And all imperfections
Of bends on our stems,
Just make us unique
In the family of man.

So thank you, dear Father,
For allowing us Life,
(Though we're obviously marked
By our periods of strife.)

Help us be useful,
Though riddled with scars;
Not God's mistakes,
But His blessings, we are!

Every day, we'll continue
To praise Him on high
And strive for perfection
In our Father's eyes.

The moral herein
Is so easy to get:
Although old and not perfect,
God's not through with us yet!

Girls' Retreat Goodbye

Life is never boring,
Always a surprise!
Who'd have thought our girls' retreat
Would end with my crossed eyes?

When I turned in bed last night,
The room before me swam.
Suddenly I was confused
To where and who I am!

Vertigo is nature's way
Of making one be still.
Just a tiny movement, and
Good grief! I'm very ill!

Could it be that I was stricken
By the dizzy spell,
Just to be reminded that
I'm still not very well?

I still have to have my rest,
Lots of liquids, too;
Try to walk a little more
Till chemo passes through.

As for our retreat this week,
What a time we've had!
God has surely blessed us all,
And leaving makes me sad.

Illness stole a day from me!
I still wanted more--
Time with insights, time for prayer,
Just what the weekend's for!

But that was just not meant to be—
I know well all the drill:
Stay in bed and chill a while;
Soon I hope I'll feel

Well enough to rejoin Life;
Good enough to smile,
Ready for some normalcy
To go another mile.

Until then, I promise
To pray for each of you.
God bless you all, I've had a ball!
But now, I bid adieu!

MAY

During the weeks after chemo, in nights when sleep evaded me, I continued my early morning vigils in the kitchen. Many mornings, I watched the sunrise lift the shade of a new day through the window of my kitchen door, as the mystery of the dark gave way to silhouettes of the familiar. Since I was now in remission, my family and friends expected me to be immediately out and about, ready to return to the race of life. But that was not the case yet. I had to be patient.

Surges of insomnia, neuropathy, and stiff joints continued to haunt me; and my energy level paralleled my low blood count. My body had undergone major changes with the surgery and subsequent weeks of chemo, and it was going to take time for it to settle into its new "normal"—whatever that turned out to be. I had to be patient.

Physical changes, however, were not the only challenge I faced on a daily basis. Emotionally, I perceived the world outside my home full of potential threats to my compromised immune system, causing me to hesitate to leave the safety of my nest. Rushing back out into a world rife with bacteria and viruses seemed quite risky. To add to that was my lack of stamina, causing any activity to leave me breathless. I had to be patient.

In the midst of regaining both my physical and emotional strength, my husband injured his knee and was facing immediate corrective surgery for a tear in his meniscus. Suddenly our roles reversed: I was now the nurse instead of the nursed, and he was the impatient patient! It was as if God knew I needed to try on my new coat of normal, to see how it would fit! Carefully, I learned how to pace myself as I once again took over the driving, the household chores, and the care-giving, pulling back when my strength ebbed to recharge with a quick nap or energizing snack. I was learning to be patient.

Patience is one virtue not embedded in my DNA. In my life before cancer, if something needed done, I wanted it done now. But this was not so for the new me. Instead of multitasking in many directions, I now focused on getting even one small project or chore done in a day and celebrated its fruition. Yet, even then, I would pay the price that night for having done it. My nightly prayers now include Patience as a daily petition to God; and, although I'm learning, it's obvious I'm still a work in progress!

Early Morn

Coffee is perking,
Blessings are counted,
Gushing like water
Over a fountain.

New day is dawning,
Breeze in the air:
God our Creator
Is everywhere.

He sits beside me,
A prayer away:
We have quite a friendship
On every day.

I tell him my worries,
I share all my pain,
His answer is growth
Of my faith once again.

He shoulders the burdens
I've had on my spirit.
My load lightens quickly
The instant He hears it.

He takes the wheel;
Only He knows the road!
I'm along for the journey,
But not in control.

O'er time He has proven
To all those who pray,
"I can't and He can!"
Just move out of the way.

He's got the solutions
He owns all the keys,
He solves hardest problems
With infinite ease.

I refill my cup,
Add cream to my brew,
Assured that God's got this
For me and for you!

Praise God in the morning,
Thank Him in the eve.
He's right there beside me
When I work or I sleep.

I don't have to worry,
I don't have to fret--
God knows the solutions,
Just not shared with me yet.

Trapped

Long illness is like memory foam:
It becomes a comfortable jail.
Each day the body sinks lower,
Between confining rails.

The deeper that I'm sinking,
The warmer is the bed,
Until one day I realize,
With all-consuming dread,

That focus on my loss of health
Has paralyzed my life;
It's as if I cannot escape
The confines of my strife!

I'm stuck between the fact I'm "healed"
But yet I'm still not whole.
The side effects that mar me
Have charged a dreadful toll.

My mind still is rejoicing
That treatment's at an end,
But my body is confused and sad
As to where my old life went.

I try to understand the reason
Of my aches, you see,
To try to analyze each pain
Intellectually;

But all that does is raise my hopes
Of feeling as I did;
But now I know I must accept
This path down which I'm led.

The doctor said he'd cure me,
And that's just what he's done:
But the cure came with the postscript
Of a body that's no fun.

The poison in my system
Extracting what was due
Was a blessing of extending life,
Yet a bane of subterfuge.

Now I must remember
To thank and praise my God
For guiding all the chemicals
That targeted my bod,

Destroying all the bad cells
To halt their rushing power--
For that I pray, each future day,
Each minute, and each hour!

And one day I will find a way
To rise up from the hole
That cancer fast has held me
And return me to my role

Of mother, spouse, and caring friend,
To family and those around me;
To redefine both stride and miles
To travel what's before me--

Not lag behind in pity,
Nor blindly run ahead,
But face the time I'm left on earth
With God nearby instead.

Praise God for all my blessings,
Praise Him for every day;
Praise Father, Son, and Holy Ghost
And all in Jesus' name!

Rose-colored Glasses

When the day dawns in glory, refreshed by night rains,
And the air is freshly perfumed;
My illness subsides, and my dreams come alive—
And my life as it was is resumed...

No, no! That's a falsehood! That thought's just untrue!
Instead, it's my hope for tomorrow!
I'm still rather puny when it comes to my health,
And this sickness is causing me sorrow.

I want to be creatively active!
With knitting and fiddling and such,
But my body won't do it, I hurt right on through it,
So do I just give it all up?

Help me, dear Father, to accept who I am,
To appreciate my time here on Earth;
I'm grateful, dear God, for the blessings and joys
Of today, from the time of my birth.

So I will continue to work on God's venue—
What He has in store for me.
There's change everywhere, of which I am aware,
So I'll accept it for posterity.

I know He is right here beside me;
I know He is holding my hand.
He helps me to cope at the end of my rope
When I haven't the courage to stand.

My cup has been chock-full of blessings—
Good childhood, good marriage, good kids,
Support from my friends—the list never ends
As I recollect all that I did.

So help me, dear Father, to recognize these
When reality overwhelms dreams;
With You near to me, the truth I can see
As I face whatever Life deems.

Preparing for Storms

I'm reading a book on the storms of our lives
And how we prepare ere they hit;
The key thought engendered
Is that we must remember
To make certain we're spiritually fit.

And how to prepare before forecasts of rain?
We follow our Lord every day
In word and in deed,
In sharing our need,
As in the calm mornings we pray.

When Life's storm has passed, and we walk on the beach,
We can see all that litters the sand.
The storm has exposed
What is already there,
Buried deep in the spirit of man.

So what can we do to keep our beach clean?
How can we lash our posts tighter?
Start each day with prayer,
Let folks know that you care,
Love your enemies to make your load lighter.

We never know what is just up ahead,
No sense using fear or denial;
Faith will strengthen your spirit,
Prayer will calm, once God hears it,
So the buffeting winds become mild.

"Peace, be still!" Jesus cried, as the boat tossed and turned;
"Do not fear!" is the mantra of Faith.
If prepared, you'll prevail,
Even with a strong gale,
If your house on the Rock you have made.

Put foundation, not heads, way down deep in the sand,
And anchor your home with your prayers.
When the mornings arise
After storms have subsided,
You will see with your eyes, God's right there.

Back to the Future

When did Life begin returning?
When did Normal move back in?
Was it when Bart's old meniscus
Of his knee gave way to pain?

Suddenly we changed our titles;
Suddenly I am the one
Lifting bags and taking trash out:
When had this great change begun?

He no longer is the strong one;
He is not behind the wheel.
I relinquished "riding shotgun,"
No matter how wiped out I feel.

Orthopedic surgeon's visit,
Surgery day marked in red;
I knew well my time of resting
Was at an end, where we were led!

Nothing changed the pain I'm feeling;
Nothing changed my nights awake.
What had changed were circumstances;
So did I, for goodness sake!

I'm the one who's now the chauffeur,
To and from his therapist;
Doing laundry, cooking supper—
No, I didn't ask for this!

When you've ridden on the tailgate
Days and weeks and months the same,
Letting others do your bidding,
Why, it's tough to take the reins!

I think God saw my complacence,
Pushed me farther from the nest,
Knowing it would make me stronger
To resume life with the rest.

Here am I, though aching sorely,
Capable in helping more.
Guess I needed a reminder
Greater things might be in store.

I had fallen into habits
That were begging remedy;
Now my husband's need is greater.
The focus is on him, not me.

So my apron is no longer
Hanging on the pantry door.
I'm a-cookin', I'm a-cleanin',
I'm a-straightnin' my kitchen drawer!

No more watching birdies feeding
Looking out my kitchen door;
Now I'm putting out the feeders
That we bought while at the store.

Payback time has caught up with me;
Time to give instead of get.
You can't get if you don't give,
So fill me up, Lord, I'm all set!

I'll continue doing daily
Practice on my violin,
Paying bills and buying groceries
As it's been since Time began.

I will also join the ranks
Of those who do for others, though;
No more passive way of living!
Active life for me's in store.

By my cancer anniversary,
I should be quite saddle sore
From climbing "back onto my horse"
And living as I was before.

With God's gentle push to urge me
Onward toward completed health,
I have realized that this is,
In Life, what's known as our true wealth.

Back again toward the future,
Letting off the brake of wife,
I accept my new assignment
In the sunset of my life.

Wherever I'm Going

"Wherever I'm going, He's already there,"
Is a good way to say that God's near me,
Not only in times when Life is awry,
But in good times as well, He can hear me.

Our Lord never moves; He is steadfast and true,
He is always waiting to calm;
When trials become harder and harder to bear,
He soothes all of my wounds like a balm.

Yet just as the veil of the troubles of man
Splits to reveal sunlight, not shade,
I have a pattern of moving away,
Disconnecting the link that we've made.

But He never leaves, just continues His vigil,
Keeping watch over me patiently;
For, without fail, when I seek Him again,
He is silently right next to me.

Good times are peppered with bad times, you see;
So our walks in His garden each day
Must always continue, no matter the venue,
And never must I turn away!

A calm is more stressful a time than a storm!
It's then that I comprehend Trust;
Not moving away in our Faith walk each day--
For Christians, an absolute must!

When the men in the boat were in fear of the storm,
Jesus commanded the water to still;
They realized with awe it was God in the boat
When the tempest died down at His will.

As I sail in my skiff, both in calm and churned waters,
When I'm seeking to reach the safe shore,
I'll let God pilot me in close proximity,
Toward the harbor that I am bound for.

Yes, wherever I'm going, I know for a fact
God will always be waiting for me.
He's already there, poised to answer my prayer
That I ask of Him, down on my knees.

JUNE

By June, my strength had not yet returned as I had hoped. When I mentioned my concern to a friend, she said I might never be the same as I had been before the cancer. This thought had never occurred to me! The purpose of chemotherapy, she added, was to heal my body of cancer, with no promises of returning me back to my former state. Accepting this as a possibility, I focused on being grateful for a second chance at life, no matter how altered the remainder may be.

On some Sundays when I still did not feel up to attending church, my mind would wander through some of the beautiful places I had worshipped during my lifetime. One memory that repeatedly came to mind was the beautiful stained glass Tiffany windows at Trinity Episcopal Church in Natchez, Mississippi, where my daughter and her family had once been members. So one day, when I drove down to Natchez to visit a friend, she took me to the church to see "my" window that had become such a symbol of faith for me.

"Christ at the Door" Tiffany window,
Trinity Episcopal Church, Natchez, MS

On some days, I returned to my violin, with little success, since much of my technique and strength had been lost during my months of my illness. The same was true of other creative outlets, such as painting and knitting. My hands just refused to cooperate, with my fingers as stiff as the needles I used for knitting. Painstakingly, I began to regain control over the bow and violin, finally resuming my lessons. Through time, I was once again able to paint a decent picture or two; the knitting, however, is still on hold!

At my first three-month checkup back in Houston, the tumor marker showed I was still cancer-free. My surgeon, however, concerned that I still was having chronic chest pain, suggested a visit to my cardiologist back in Alexandria. After running some tests, he found a blockage in one artery, immediately correcting it with a stent. Having both cancer and heart disease discovered and treated during the same year was providential, not accidental: God was always by my side!

My Old Black Cat

I dreamed about my old black cat
That I shared with my sister.
Her tail was broke, her eyes were blind,
Her meow was a whisper.
Her glossy coat that lost its sheen
Had turned a dull, drab brown;
But her spirit held a sparkle
That, to us, made her reknown!

When a stray dog climbed the wooden steps
That led to our back door,
She'd slide down from her lofty perch
And hobble across the floor.
With sightless eyes, she'd follow sound,
Straight up in his direction;
With all her strength, she'd mount the dog
With aerial perfection!

""Yee hah!" The cat would dig her claws
Into the puppy's hide;
And hanging on for dear life,
Off our back yard, she'd ride,
Until at last the dog escaped
From claws embedded deep,
And headed home as fast
As little doggy feet could keep!

Yes, Momma Cat's a heroine
From all my childhood days!
She taught me how to "just hold on"
When bad times seemed to stay.
With a little perseverance,
Even though she was so frail,
My Momma Cat stood strong
From her bald head to her broke tail!

And I, now in my cancered state,
With baldness, aches, and pain,
Am urged forth through the memory
Of her riding, once again.
If she could stay on bareback
Of a running, yelping pup,
I'm sure I can, as well, hold on
Through all that Life sends up!

There are examples all around us
In our corner of the world
To give us just the impetus
We need for strength unfurled.
So recognize the traits around
In mundane things we see,
To help get through the trials we face,
Through our adversity.

"All creatures great and small"
Seem to have humanistic traits
That bring to mind ourselves,
When things are put upon our plates.
"If they can do it, so can we!"
Becomes our battle call!
Because they're "wise and wonderful"
They're examples to us all.

Yes, kitty cats and puppy dogs,
And mice and snakes and birds
May offer us a pattern
For our lives, much more than words.
So thanks to Mother Nature,
In partnership with God,
For helping us to see ourselves
On all our paths we trod.

O Lord, Will You Forgive Me?

O Lord, will You forgive me?
I think I lost my way.
I stayed the path while things were good
And rarely did I stray.

But soon as boulders blocked the road,
I stopped and wrung my hands,
Instead of holding one of yours--
I do not understand.

I know that You're my Comforter;
I know that You love me;
So why, in times of deep distress,
You, God, did I not seek?

Instead, I sat beside the path
Next to the rock and cried;
I feasted on the Fear I found,
And from it, my Faith died.

I know that Fear's the enemy;
I know that Faith's the friend.
Both cannot live together,
So which lasts to the end?

Of course, the answer's easy:
It's Faith that moves the mountains!
Why does that Truth seem hard to me
When I need to surmount them?

It's just that Fear erases
My spiritual good sense,
And in Faith's place, replaces it
With nothing for defense.

Forgive me, O my Father,
That I stumbled and I fell;
I promise to keep trying, Lord,
While following the trail

That you have set before me,
That you have walked along
Beside me just to be my Guide
And help me to stay strong.

My soul just needs a band-aid
When I have hit a wall,
I know that for your first-aid kit,
I only need to call.

I'm sure that I'm forgiven,
Because I've asked you to;
But now I must forgive myself
For it to all come true.

I praise you for my blessings,
That grow along the way;
I praise you for my godly friends
Who pray for me each day.

I praise you for your only Son
Who died for all our sins;
And most of all, I praise You, Lord,
For being my best friend.

So may I walk beside You
On this rocky stretch of land
And feel Your gentle presence
As I reach to hold Your hand?

Together we will go the way
You have prepared for me
And climb up to the summit's crest
Toward Eternity.

Try, Try Again

When we've done the rounds of chemo,
When we've mastered every test,
And been shown a hearty "thumbs up,"
Thus relieving all the stress;

Yet the imaging shows hot spots
That upset me, I confess--
Can You scoot a little closer, Lord,
And be with me through the rest?

Yes, I know You're right beside me;
I have never doubted You;
But I don't know how to listen
During trials we're walking through.

Conversations loudly screaming
In my heart and in my head
Are demanding my attention,
Drowning out Your voice instead.

As Your words are calmly whispered,
Filled with comforting peace,
I'm relying on my headphones
To make all this chaos cease!

Please, be patient, Lord, I'm trying!
Hold me when I pull away!
I'm not ready yet to leave this earth--
I want some other days!

I still need to iron some wrinkles out
Of my now rumpled state,
Use my Bible as my guidebook,
Wipe some issues off the slate.

I want to know You better,
'Ere your neighbor I will be,
When we'll walk the streets together
In your heaven eternally!

So, from hence forth, I will praise You!
Yes, my future prayer will be
To become a better person,
As You unconditionally

Love me as I metamorph
Into what You've planned for me.
It takes courage, it takes patience,
But, with Your help, I will see

On the day I bow before You,
(Humbly lowering my eyes),
I will glide toward Perfection
Only You can recognize.

So, for now, please stand beside me,
Calm my oh, so quivering stance,
Give me strength to face my treatments,
Quiet my vocal raves and rants.

Let me be a kinder person
To my family helping me,
Recognizing they are serving
As Your earthly hands and feet.

Thank you, Lord, for all my blessings,
Praising You for all You've done,
Prayerfully, I'll follow closely
As with faith I'll travel on.

The Window of Comfort

The darkened church was hushed and close,
Its holiness profound,
When we two slipped into the room
Without a single sound.

I made my way across the floor,
Drawn by the glorious sight
Of *Christ at the Door* to welcome me,
Its brilliant glass alight.

This was a pilgrimage for me,
One that I'd hoped to take
All through my months of illness--
Now I was here, to give God praise.

"Just take your time," you whispered,
As you softly closed the door.
You knew I needed time alone
To talk to my dear Lord.

I stood and stared into His face,
That rays of sun highlighted;
His kindly eyes, his gentle smile--
The visage of Almighty!

How in the world did Tiffany
Take softly colored glass
And quilt the pieces fused by lead
Into such wondrous mass!

The window told God's story.
Its beauty squeezed my heart!
It beckoned me to follow Him
So never will we part.

I knelt, as the kaleidoscope
Of color dazzled me.
The holy aura round His face
Was such a sight to see!

Its homily was crystal clear,
Its message so revealing!
There, I received a blessing
While quietly kneeling.

My months of illness dropped away,
My eyes were brimmed with tears.
I pulled myself up awkwardly,
While sensing Him so near.

I silently reversed my way,
Back to the exit door,
Where you, my friend, were waiting,
While I'd found what I came for.

I turned around for one more glance
Before I closed the doorway,
Fluorescence of the lighted hall
Was no match for such glory!

Yes, worshipping our Father
May transpire in many ways:
The sound of priest and glorious choir,
The sight of sunlit rays

That filter through the fiery glass,
The mellow stain of wood;
The tactile feel of kneeling bench
Or carpet where we stood.

The smell of incense rising high
And candles burning low,
The tangy taste of wine and bread
All mesh together so.

But today, I know my blessing
Was to see *Christ at the Door*;
As I've seen it in my mind's eye
For at least nine months or more.

Each Sunday I'd envision it
While I worshipped from my bed,
Since I was not quite able
To go to church instead.

God, thank you for my patient friend
Who knew my heart was pained
And took me to the church,
So I could find my way again.

Gathering Dust

My paints and canvas gather dust,
My knitted sock's not done;
The violin is still and mute:
Am I the only one

Who made it through the chemo
And out the other side,
Yet can't resume life as before,
Because the pain won't die?

The doctors I conferred with
Suggested several pills;
I took them at my bedtime,
Yet even felt more ill!

I prayed that You would intervene
And take the pain away;
But guess Your answer to me is
There's reason it should stay.

So what am I to learn from this--
A cleansing of the soul?
Is this my bed of nails to rid
Me of my sins untold?

I know that I'm impatient;
I know it could be worse--
But, God, can we just talk it out
After You fix it first?

My life has always centered
On creativity;
So maybe You just think I need
To focus outwardly

On more important issues
That are happening all around,
Instead of pen and bow and paint
To keep me more aground.

It may be time to put away
These items of my art
And study tomes to better me
E're it's too late to start!

I look into the future--
It's veiled in mystery;
I look into the past as well--
My personal history.

I'm such a tiny little speck
On Earth's rotating sphere;
A cloak of insignificance
Is what I seem to wear.

The teeny light inside my soul
May not be very bright,
But when it's joined by others' glow,
'It gives a lovely light.'

It may just make a difference
To illuminate the Way
For others who are moving toward
The path we need to take

That leads to our Eternal Home
Where all is bright and clear,
Where we'll reside forever,
With You, my God, so near.

So, Lord, will You please clarify
My purpose on this earth
And help me understand how pain
Intensifies its worth?

If it's Your wish that it will be
A part of my tomorrow,
Then help me to accept it now
Without a hint of sorrow.

Yet, if in time, You choose that I
May once again be free
Of all its inconsistencies--
That'll be just fine with me!

Cancer and Heart?

First, cancer--and now, my heart?
The chemo, then a stent?
Goodness gracious, do you know
Just where my good health went?

It seems like just a week ago
That I was in my prime;
But guess it surely must have been
A little longer time.

Where is the girl who juggled
A baby on each hip,
While cooking, playing, cleaning
Without a single slip?

Where is the one who taught all day,
Then added more degrees,
Who wrote and illustrated books
With obvious ease?

And then she lived with grandkids
When their dad was very ill,
Trading sides of desk without due rest,
Keeping kids until

Their parents got to come home;
And then she crossed the sea
To visit England with her son--
Was that woman really me?

Today I'm just the shadow
Of who I was before,
With cancer first, then heart disease,
With aches and pains galore!

I look into the mirror
To try to recognize
The old one who is staring back--
I only know her eyes.

I've lost my vim and vigor,
My straight, fine hair, my zeal;
And in their place, I pray to God,
I'll one day fill the bill

With energy from my new stent
And from the chemo gone,
With hope reborn inside my frame
To keep me keeping on.

I need my patience that I dropped
Somewhere along the way;
I also need my stamina
I lost another day.

I pray that soon I'll play a tune
On my discarded fiddle
(That sounds more like a mad burro
Squeezed tightly round its middle!)

I want to go to church again,
With husband next to me,
Since church on television
Doesn't feed me spiritually.

Please find my patience, Lord, I ask!
I know I'm almost there.
The road's been long, I'm getting strong,
And know You're close as prayer.

I thank You for Your healing touch;
I thank You for my friends;
I thank You for my family
Who always to me tends.

Don't want to forget kindnesses
I've gotten from above;
Or fall into a deep, dark place
I struggle to climb from.

I thank you, Lord, for blessings
I name before I sleep,
And if I die before I wake,
I pray my soul to keep.

JULY

Summertime set in with a fury of night sweats, stiff joints, and more sleepless nights; yet, in tiny steps, I knew I was getting better. Ever so often, I would awaken with a vigor I had not felt since the surgery; yet other days, I began to wonder if the cancer had returned. During the nights, I continued writing poems that had become more of a running stream-of-conscious dialogue with God.

I was impatient with my slow progress and all the impediments to getting better. I needed exercise but couldn't do so with the neuropathy in my feet, for fear of falling. I wanted to play the violin or paint, but the stiffness in my hands did not allow it. Through these challenges, however, I was learning some valuable lessons of life.

Always a problem solver, I tried to dissect the pain and study it, attempting to understand why it occurred at certain times, but not at others. I tried to recount what I had done during the previous day that might have triggered the night's specific problem. I looked for patterns of pain, in terms of the weather or my day's activities. But the conclusion as to why it was continuing so long was no clearer than before.

Chemo leaves its imprint on the body that may not ever be totally erased, as each body reacts in its own individual way to the drug. It is a foreign matter that the delicate network of our body must learn to accept or reject, as it works its magic to destroy the deadly cancer cells. Some of the neighboring healthy cells, however, may be damaged as well in the process, which is the price we must pay to be cured.

That left only one thing: Acceptance. No more questions why. Just what is. Get on with Life. Be grateful for all the blessings each day. Learn to say no, if faced to activities too great to tackle. Breathe. Pause. Relax. Accept. Embrace my new normal.

With the uncertainty of the future, and my newfound, ill-fitting cloak of acceptance, I needed more assurance. So I turned to the textbook of God—my Bible. Although I always read the Bible during my devotions, I now searched the scripture for different themes: death, heaven, and, yes, even acceptance. The Psalms brought me particular pleasure, when I identified that half were lamentations and the rest were filled with praise—just like my poems!

Lessons Learned

Some nights the pain is really bad,
And this one takes the cake.
When it lets up, I'll be so glad,
Its power o'er me break.

For now, however, I will sit
In darkened kitchen chair.
It's possible, when daylight breaks,
You may still find me there.

When I awake with nerves on fire,
With muscles aching deeply,
I struggle to get up awhile
To stretch them and get sleepy.

My hands won't let me write or knit;
My hips won't let me rise
Without a lot of effort,
Tears brimming in my eyes.

I try to read a calming book
To soothe my tired state;
But letters do not form the words
When all my body aches.

So after hours have stiffly marched
Where I have sat the night,
I try to go on back to bed
To sleep til morning light.

I pray that God will gently hum
A lullaby for me,
To stir inside a slower pulse,
To rock me peacefully.

I trust Him to restore my health
As chemo ebbs away,
So that I may feel once again
As I did yesterday.

I know that there are lessons in
These nightly hours of pain,
I just don't fancy doing this
Again, and then again.

Experiential learning
Is easier, they say,
If it's not manifested
With pains along the way.

By now, my body knows the moves
To this macabre dance,
At least I know the rhythm
And can shuffle through the stance.

God's with me while I'm feeling low,
He's still here when I'm fine.
I've learned hard lessons through it all,
As shown here in my rhyme.

Acceptance

I've never known Acceptance well;
I've fought it all my days.
I tend to turn my face away
And ignore it when it stays.

It must be great to be an owl,
Whose head can turn one-eighty!
Because when my denial speaks,
My neck feels rather weighty!

To face the issues Life can bring
Requires a strength of will
That I do not seem to possess
Without just "being still."

For when I cease my frantic pace
Both in my brain and out,
I feel the close proximity
Of my most gracious God.

My energy has left the house,
Residing in my dreams;
And in its place, a void has formed
Inside my inner me.

I wonder if the time will come
When I will evermore
Know what it is to feel again
With energy restored?

I keep on looking down the road,
To see if I'm all healed,
Still drowning in denial that
This is the best I'll feel.

So here's when old Acceptance
Has reared its ancient head.
"Come follow me," it says to me,
"And I'll show you how instead

To live your life as God expects,
To find a peace of mind;
It may not be what you had picked,
But what God's plan defined."

I take God's hand, as I accept
The wonders hidden there;
For wrapped in all my problems
Are God's promises so rare!

As we walk toward tomorrow,
But staying in the now,
My path gets smoother every step
My spirit will allow.

For on this path next to my Lord
I finally feel the peace,
That God has promised as a gift
When all resistance ceased.

The Good Book

Another night of sitting up;
Can't sleep for all the pain.
Will I be ever able
To sleep all night again?

By eight, my lids are heavy,
So I turn out the light;
But two hours past, I'm up again—
When will I be all right?

My sleep patterns are crazy!
There is no rhyme or reason.
It really doesn't matter,
Which week or month or season.

The pain is not a consequence
Of what I ate for dinner;
If I'd quit eating every guess,
I'd certainly be thinner.

My hands and feet are stiffer;
Joints don't bend as before.
It's difficult to flex my toes
For feeling to restore.

"My Father, can you handle this?"
I bow my head and pray.
"Please tell me what will soothe the pain:
That's what I ask today."

And then I see my Bible
Next to my rocking chair,
Containing all the answers
God has provided there.

I finger through the Good Book
And choose a favorite verse
To help me navigate through time
When I am at my worst.

I come upon a passage
I once had underlined
And made a side notation
When it was read last time.

Years earlier, it had helped me
To weather other storms
That thundered loudly through my life,
At night or early morn.

And, oh, look, there's another!
And yet, a third one, too!
There are so many passages
For God to get me through!

I feel I'm getting drowsy;
The pain has let me go,
As I have wandered through His words
He spoke so long ago.

I take my reading glasses off,
And turn off all the lights—
My Comforter has comforted;
So I bid you good night.

Death

I've thought a lot about my death
And my mortality,
Since I've been ill for several months,
I'm still unclear, you see.

It sometimes seem a tiny step
From one life to the other,
And, yes, I know how thrilled I'll be
To see my dad and mother;

But since my earthly family
And friends still love me so,
It's hard to turn away from them
And break away to go.

Heaven must be wonderful!
The Bible tells me so.
I know that I'll be whole again,
And that's so nice to know.

And never will I shed a tear.
No sadness will there be;
Instead, I'll have tranquillity
To live in, peacefully.

I don't quite get the "streets of gold,"
Because I won't need wealth;
They frankly don't appeal to me—
I only need my health.

But while I'll stay upon this earth,
I'll grow in faith some more;
So when my time arrives to leave,
I'll step on through the door.

My sister, on her deathbed,
Said, "How do you 'Let go'?
There are no instructions here,
At least, none that I know!"

Yet when the angel took her hand
And led her to the Light,
I remember thinking
How she seemed to do it right!

I only know that's where I want
To be forevermore;
I'll try to live a life of faith,
Since I know what's in store.

The past few months, I've had more time
To walk and talk with God,
And when I visit Him in prayer,
I feel a heavenly nod.

I'll live forever after!
I know just where I'll be,
When once we step across the veil,
My Father God and me.

A Glimpse of Heaven

I caught a glimpse of heaven,
When yesterday, the pain
Was gone for several hours,
Yet then returned again.

For several shining moments,
I was as once before!
Oh, God, how wonderful it was
When my health was restored!

For months now, I've been burdened
With aches from head to toe,
I hardly recognized myself
As I was long ago!

Not only did the pain recede,
My confidence returned.
A rolling tide of energy
Throughout my body surged.

I suddenly was able
To do things as before.
In retrospect, it almost seemed
My body was reborn.

And in the sunlight of it all,
I set my mind to climb
The mound of paperwork that I'd
Put off for later times.

Within a few short hours,
I'd quickly finished, then
I pushed my chair back from the desk
And loudly capped my pen.

My energy was shimmering,
My aches were dancing near;
So I lay down and fell asleep—
And then, just as I'd feared,

When I awoke, I could not move
My paralytic frame.
The pain had taken hold once more—
I hurt and ached again!

It was as if my time was up
To see into Tomorrow;
And yet, it had been such a gift,
I didn't feel great sorrow.

I know that I may once again
Be as I was before;
My lack of pain will come and go
Like waves upon the shore.

And with each one, I will regain
Some of my old self back!
And I will hopefully emerge
With strength that I now lack.

It's just as if God granted me
A telescopic look
Of what's ahead, so I won't dread
New chapters in my book.

Don't throw away my paints and brush,
My violin, my knitting!
Just keep them all real close at hand,
Nearby where I'll be sitting.

As the pain-free times appear,
I'll use those precious minutes
So that, as days give way to weeks,
I'll finish projects in it.

To God, I offer praise and thanks.
My gratitude o'erflowing;
For all the blessings from above
Especially for showing

The possibilities You wrought
Within my sickened frame,
To give me hope tomorrow that
I'll be pain-free again.

Awake at Seven

I just awoke at seven
Am trying to unbend.
I stayed awake from twelve to three—
I couldn't sleep again.

The pain was on a zip line
From my head down to my toes.
And when I tried to stand upright,
A lightning bolt arose.

I have my own alarm clock
That's deep inside of me.
I only need to move a bit
For it to start to ring.

It signals when my day begins
With stretching calisthenics
To loosen up my stiffened frame
And all that aches within it.

It may well be at midnight
Or early in the morn.
Time doesn't matter when it hurts—
I roll out with a yawn.

I read a while, I pray a while,
A puzzle for my head;
But when I get my sleepy back,
I go back to my bed.

Then as the morn arises,
Although I'm still so tired,
I don my robe and slippers
And get the cook stove fired.

My joints that ache as I awake
Are mutely telling me
They've had enough of lying down
And want some hot coffee!

It's not the way I wish to wake
Each morning from now on,
But guess it signals that I'm still
Alive to watch the dawn.

The sunrise is, with ribboned sky,
A gift from my Creator,
A present for my getting up
Much sooner than much later.

He knows my days begin with pain
And offers it to soothe,
So thank you, God, for colored skies
In every brilliant hue.

AUGUST

Looking back over the collection of poems I wrote, it is evident that I was becoming stronger both physically and spiritually as each calendar page was discarded. Although there are still times of doubt and fear and uncertainty, for the most part, my life is returning to a level I can tolerate.

One of the gifts of the year has been my ability to view the outside world with heightened awareness of God's creation. I now am more conscious of seeing the parallels between the antics of birds and people. During the day, I see the palate of color and patterns of nature as never before; while at night, the moon and stars appear to shine more brightly in the heavens. Even on rainy nights, the rhythm of the rain sounds more comforting than before. It is as if my eyes and ears were opened wider to the "beauty of the earth" and the "glory of the skies", to use the well-chosen words of an old hymn. And for every living thing and each precious moment, I say a prayer of "grateful praise."

My time away from the world has made me a wiser person. Since I've always loved to learn, I received my undergraduate degree in my '20's, my master's in my '40's, and, as I was smelling sixty, my doctorate only years before retirement. This year, however, I learned the most important lessons of all--about life, love, and living during the physical and emotional struggles of a debilitating illness.

After my retirement eight years ago, I wanted to tackle some of the items on my bucket list. So an old family violin was brought out of the back of a closet for lessons, while a friend offered her skill of how to knit as well. But these were skills of creativity, things to do to make life more fun and full and focused. What I learned through my year with cancer, however, was more profound--learning to persevere in adversity; learning to see God in every place, feeling, and thought; studying the word of God, not only as a guide to both living and dying. Through this year, I have gained a deeper understanding of faith, trust, acceptance, and love. How I live my life from this time forth will prove how much I have grown spiritually.

Mind Games

After my lengthy illness,
In times of feeling sick,
My confidence just plummets,
So needs a little kick!

Is it my imagination
That I'm feeling rather "off"?
My stomach lurches to my throat;
I feel the need to cough.

Maybe hypochondria
Is catching up with me.
Or has my cancer reappeared
Inside my scarred tummy?

Could it be a side effect
Of all the chemo taken,
Or is it just my mind at work,
Since cancer's left me shaken?

I tend to try to figure out
What triggers these attacks;
But all I seem to get from it
Are codes that I can't crack.

Does it actually matter
What's the cause to the effect?
Well, yes, if it is possible that
The cancer's coming back!

It's probably quite normal
To feel the fear once more,
When my mind wanders on ahead,
Predicting what's in store.

I must reel in these faithless thoughts!
I must stay in the Now!
I cannot, will not, move ahead:
This I shall not allow!

For God is with me through my fears
To bolster up my faith.
And calmly must I recollect:
"Be still," my God hath saith.

So back to bed to rest awhile,
Slow down and meditate;
I can't surrender to my God
When I am in this state.

Both faith and fear cannot reside
Inside my body twain;
I must decide which one I'll keep
And which I will abstain.

With faith, I can move mountains;
With fear, I dip so low.
The answer to this quandary
Is an easy one to know!

And as I count my blessings,
Each day, since God is near,
The healing He has wrought for me
Is absolutely clear.

So I will hold this positive thought
In center of my being,
As I lay down to rest tonight--
What peace He is revealing!

I thank God for my blessings,
My cup has runneth o'er!
I will forever praise His name
From now to evermore.

Sometimes

Sometimes heartache erases
Our times that are no more;
It is as if God scrubs us clean
Of lives that were before.

Sometimes He takes the skin clean off,
Since love has gone so deep,
But other times He polishes it
So beautifully, we weep.

Sometimes we feel the hurt so strong,
We think it's an attack!
Our heart is bleeding from within,
And there's no going back!

But as the hour passes,
God applies His healing balm
To close the wounds of yesterday—
A blessing like a psalm.

For although we can't see ahead,
And know what's going to be,
God knows our lives from birth to death,
Into Eternity.

We simply trust His guiding hand
To lead us through our days;
He comforts in the rough times, and
He helps in countless ways.

By noticing the blessings
Each night before we dream,
We praise Him for all that He's done,
And will still do again.

Just stay within this block of time
And don't rush up ahead,
Creating conversations
Inside our fear-filled heads.

But follow in His footsteps.
He'll carry us a bit
When times are rough, and daily stuff
Makes us not feel too fit.

Until one morn, the sunlight streams
Into our shuttered hearts,
And joy unfettered beckons us,
And happiness restarts!

We've come out on the other side,
We've left the cavern dark,
And now are facing rainbows and
The calling of a lark.

And if we look back to the path
We've followed, rife with tears,
We also notice flowers
Where once the dust appeared.

As we had walked through hard days,
God lifted up our spirits,
So that, since we are happy now,
We'll tell all who can hear it.

"God saw me through the bad times
And then erased the pain;
He'll be always right next to me--
I'll never doubt again!"

We know when Life forces a change
We cannot overthrow,
We simply reach out for His hand
And forward we will go.

With trust and faith and daily praise,
We journey on our way,
Until we see the Master
Who has been our Guide each day.

Morning Soliloquy

As I sit and drink my coffee
And watch the sun arise,
I witness a true metaphor
Right before my eyes.

The hummingbirds are swarming
Round the feeder on the porch.
They seem to know what time to come
Before the sun has scorched

The flowers in the garden,
The grass that browns from heat--
The feeder is their respite,
As well as where they eat.

Their human characteristics
Are noticeable when
They bicker, and they poke their beaks
To push away their friends.

One little bird looks ruffled;
He's angry every day.
He chases off the others
If they get into his way.

It's obvious that he's disliked
By all the other peers.
They seem to talk about him
As they swarm and as they jeer.

A little like, in middle school,
Where the strong attacks the weak.
There's always been a kid or two
Who gets stuck with a beak!

Until each finds self-confidence
To stand up to the bully,
The gangs will all continue
To taunt the weak ones fully.

But soon, with every push and shove,
All get a soothing sip;
Then circling the feeder,
And off in just a zip.

One lap around the big oak tree,
A rest upon the bush,
Then back they come to feed again,
With poke and shove and push.

So what can humans learn from them?
For nature is our teacher.
Those birds are in survival mode;
Example is our preacher.

We all can choose to spend our days
Just pushing and complaining,
Or we can wait until our turn,
Or fill up when it's raining.

Either way, we meet our goal,
Tho one is more genteel;
It's nice when we let others know
Exactly how we feel.

The mean, old bird now sits on guard
To keep them all away;
He's got his way for one more time—
Not worth it, I would say.

He's friendless, making days grow long,
He's fat from all the food;
A couch potato of a bird,
A life that is not good.

So may we learn a lesson
From all our birdie fellows:
When life keeps poking at you,
Be kind, be sweet, be mellow!

Praise to our God the Father,
Praise to His Holy Son,
Who made the birds we can enjoy:
We're blessed by every one!

Mortality

When viewing our mortality
While sick upon the bed,
It's almost like a mirrored view
From our birth till our death.

We feel the brush of angel wings,
The pull of Dad and Mother;
Yet we are safely grounded here
Among all our loved others.

Our body is both twixt and tween,
In this life and the next;
It seems uncertain where it needs
To focus and direct.

We often think we drive our fate,
But that's all just a ruse;
It's God that is the One-in-Charge:
Life's not just what we choose.

There is a wide, uncertain place
Where we can't see the ending.
Our bodies, still not healed yet,
Are quietly mending.

But other chronic problems
Have raised their ugly heads,
Creating major roadblocks
That keep us in our beds.

That's when it's hardest to accept;
It's when I start to doubt—
Am I going to make it through,
Or has my time run out?

Just focus on today, my friend;
Just one step, then another.
Remember all the baby steps
You took beside your mother.

Let God direct and hold you tight,
The aches may soon abate;
(You only have control to change
The channels that you hate!

Don't spend your time with worrying;
Instead, make every day
Become the best it's meant to be
In faith along the way.

Do what the doctor tells you;
And what your spouse says, too.
Give thanks for every hint of good
In all you try to do.

Time will continue onward,
And you'll go with the flow;
Before long you will realize
You're better than you know.

Anniversary Waltz

I can't believe it's been a year;
It seems more like a doz,
Since Dr. Burge discovered
The tumor where it was.

He sent me to get blood work;
He sent me for a scan;
He sent me for an ultrasound,
Then to come back again.

Each time I left and then returned
To sit inside my cell,
My fear was growing palpable,
The air was growing stale.

I felt his concern deepen
As each test proved him right—
This was the bleak beginning
Of the trial of my life!

He gently hugged me as I left,
A tactile benediction.
I felt my world turn upside down
Beyond my recognition.

The second opinion led us
Down to Houston town,
And within days, my garb had changed
To a plain hospital gown.

My son and brother came to help,
With daughter, at my side—
Through surgery and chemo,
To make the cancer die.

One friend from Memphis sat with me;
A friend from Natchez prayed,
And gave me mantras to get through
The ragged nights and days.

My name was put on prayer lists
From every church and steeple;
I keenly felt the power
In the prayers of the people!

Our mailbox sagged from all the cards;
Cathedral candles lit
On both sides of the ocean
For God to make me fit.

They all supported Bart and me
As we traversed the trail
Of chemo, pain, and home again,
A pendulum of hell.

Sometimes friends bought our groceries,
Some made a tasty dish,
Just trying to get me to eat,
To cook whatever I wished.

Another brought boiled custard,
A tasty treat indeed;
While others called or texted me
To find out what we need.

I've been so fortunate to have
Two friends in ministry.
One came by to visit,
While the other texted me.

The weeks blurred into months until
I was deemed cancer-free—
I thought I'd be my old self
Almost immediately.

But side effects had taken hold
Of my spirit and my pain;
So I'm not sure, even till this day,
If I'll be whole again.

The chemo kept its promise:
The cancer is no more,
But in the process, changed my health
And made my body sore.

And each day I'm reminded
Of the blessing I've been given
Through God and friends and medicine—
I've seen a glimpse of heaven!

Through many a sleepless, achy night
My spiritual thoughts grow deep
As I study and I pray
To get me back to sleep.

And through it all, my husband
Has been a strength to me;
This year has been our toughest one
Out of almost fifty.

So when I count my blessings,
It takes a little while.
(If I lined them on a highway,
They would need an extra mile!)

I've been given, through this year apart,
Time to think and time to grow,
Having solitude to recognize
What I truly need to know.

Not many get this option,
So I thank God for time
To spend in talking with Him
Or to pen a little rhyme,

Always focused on eternity
And my constant journey there.
I now know just where I'm headed
Without any trace of fear.

Praise God for all my blessings,
Both in heaven and earth below;
For His Son and Holy Spirit
Through which all these blessings flow.

POSTLUDE

After a year has passed, I still am hampered by the osteoarthritis and neuropathy that plague me. After stretching and walking around the house, however, the discomfort usually becomes manageable enough for me to get on with my day. I still feel discouraged at times; but, all in all, Life is settling down.

The week before my September checkup, Hurricane Harvey hit Houston with a vengeance, temporarily closing M D Anderson Cancer Center. Since the last checkup, my daughter had moved from southern Louisiana to eastern Oklahoma, making the drive to Houston an even longer one. We faced the upcoming trip with uncertainty of not only the flooded roads, but also of what we would find upon our arrival. Since we knew there would be many people there in need of aid, we purchased several prepaid credit cards to hand out. What we received in return was overwhelming humility.

During the year of my recovery, my husband's memory loss had become more noticeable to us and more bothersome to him. Years before, when he had contracted West Nile virus while hiking, never did we dream that, as a side effect, dementia would strike him years later. But it did. So our trip to Houston now had two purposes: my checkup for cancer at M D Anderson and his testing for dementia at the Baylor College of Medicine. We had successfully weathered one storm and now were heading directly into another.

Returning to Houston the following month for his tests to be read, our trip was a little more exciting than most. Driving down to Houston on a Sunday, we stopped for gas, only to be surprised when the car would not start again. At the gas station on the side of a deserted Texas highway, we called for our car to be towed to a dealership in the next town, checked in to a retro motel next door, ate our supper at a local diner, and ordered a rental car to drive to Houston the next day. It was no coincidence that all of our needs that day had been met on the side of a highway bisecting a deserted stretch of land. The following day, arriving at our appointment with only ten minutes to spare, we met with our doctors, reversed our direction, and made it back in time to pick up our car and turn in the rental car before closing time. It was an unbelievable example that God was with us!

These days, I count the passage of time by my quarterly checkups in Houston and am growing stronger physically each month. Now it is my turn to help my husband, just as he helped me during my bout of cancer and treatments. God's timing was perfect, giving me a year to heal before we needed to switch jobs from caregiver to patient and vice versa. I know, with God's help, we will be able to cope with his illness, just as we did with mine. Thanks be to God!

Clicking Fingers

I now have clicking fingers
To add to my distress,
They're stiffest in the morning
After a night of rest.

I cannot hold my coffee cup;
My talons will not bend;
It takes a while to mind my brain,
From whence the message sent.

I've soaked them in warm water;
I've covered them with lotion;
I've even thought of swallowing
A dose of witch's potion!

During the day, I try to play
My violin a little,
But the encumbrance of my hands
Turns it into a fiddle!

I tried to write some thank you notes
That needed to be written;
The scrawls upon the paper looked
More like tracks of a kitten!

I've now put up my paints and brush,
My pens and inks and such—
The blotched results I end up with
Do not impress me much.

Reminds me of the elephant
I saw on Internet
Who paints with her proboscis--
That's the result I get!

I've had to take my wedding rings
Off of my gnarled hand.
No longer can I get them on,
Not even the narrow band.

I guess it may get better,
But more and more, it seems
Some things that chemo gave me
Will keep on lingering.

I have to face the truth I see
And just keep moving on;
(At least my fingers still are good
At texting on the phone!)

I still can hold my husband's hand
Or scratch an itchy spot,
And those are both necessities
To enjoy the life I've got.

So I thank you, Father, for my hands,
Even when they're feeling stiff,
I'll try to find creative ways
To grasp and write and lift.

But, all in all, I know I'm blessed
With what they can still do,
As I fold my hands devotedly
And say a prayer to You.

Throughout This Year

Throughout this year, you've been right here
To help me through it all.
I have to say, there's not a day
Goes by, that you don't call.

That makes me feel important;
That makes me feel beloved,
That you would take time for my sake
To stay close as a glove!

You send me good devotionals
Of positivity;
They're social meditations
That mean so much to me.

I know I can be honest
To tell you how I feel;
And, likewise, you can say to me
What you perceive as real.

You pull the focus from myself
To where it needs to be,
So that I've perspective
Of the world, and not just me.

I must not be the center
Of all my thoughts and tasks!
I must give wholly of myself
So my compassion lasts.

A narcissistic view of life
Is not what we should live,
So I will try, as time goes by,
To give all I can give,

To show my Christian values,
By sharing, as you do,
By putting God as Number One
And others, Number Two.

So thanks for your example
Of living for the Lord.
With God beside you every day
Entrusting in His Word.

And soon someday I can repay
All you have done for me.
I thank you for your friendship—
God's been so good to me!

Introspection

My health has imprisoned
My body and mind.
It's like I'm not able
To step over the line

Twixt recuperation
And being quite ill;
Just wish I could locate
A magical pill!!

This year I have stayed in
And took all the meds;
I even resorted
To long hours in bed.

I kept away friends
Who had wanted to come
To bring a hot dinner
The miles to my home.

My phone was the only way
That I connected;
Some friends didn't see
They weren't being rejected!

I know there are those
Who stay ill for much longer,
As well as the many
Who never get stronger.

I'm extremely grateful
To God on His Throne
That He never, no never
Has left me alone.

And the chemo has cured me
So far as the cancer—
But there are still a few questions
That need to be answered:

Is my time up, I wonder,
On this beautiful earth
Where I've had a good life
Since the moment of birth?

Am I fading away,
Just one day at a time,
Yet moving my focus
Toward the Light that's sublime?

Is this shifting direction
Causing my world to tilt?
Is that why it's no longer
Well that I've felt?

Dear Father, I want
To be perfectly clear:
I'm not quite yet ready
To leave my life here.

There is so much more
That I still want to do
In your Name, here on earth,
To bring others to You.

I think if I manage
To locate some pep,
I might learn to be able
To take longer steps

Toward a rejuvenation
Of body and mind,
(And untangle the nerves
That have not been too kind!)

I thank God for all
Of the blessings received,
For the curing of cancer
That's happened in me—

So stay close beside me,
I'll try not to wander,
As the pathway to wellness
Continues to flounder.

And, hopefully, soon
Down the road, round the bend,
I'll recover completely—
And these poems will end!!

Saturday Morning

Saturday morning is my time to take
My weekly chaos and transform it straight.
Laundering all of the clothes that were worn,
Addressing old problems and thoughts newly born.

It is an end to the five days of normal,
It is a slowing of hours immortal;
Coffee and dressing and moving so fast
Relax that day into a comfortable mass.

And after the pause of our Saturday morn,
There's still afternoon that is spread out before,
A vista of smiles, just ready to break
As we rejuvenate with this time that we take.

Even the evening gives benediction
To our week behind us we lived with conviction!
A dinner for two, or a roasted hot dog
While swatting mosquitoes astride a cut log.

It's as if we've cleaned out the clog in the drain,
Bathed off the dust in the sweet falling rain;
Now, as we're tucked in our clean-sheeted beds,
Peace habitating both our hearts and our heads,

We're now prepared for our worship tomorrow!
To climb the church steps, less burdened with sorrow.
Ready to pray in those hushed, hallowed seats,
Starting our new week with infinite ease.

Yes, Saturday is a sweet pause in our plan,
A day of retreat to revive us again,
Time to review the week that has just passed,
Getting prepared for the next week's new tasks.

So take a deep breath, and let it exhale.
Fill up your mug and answer your mail;
It's your vacation of sorts for your bod—
An ongoing present from our Father God.

Preparations

I feel the unease mounting
As I start to make my list
Of all I must take with us
As I return for tests.

I always fear I will forget
A signed permission slip,
And then be told to go back home
To Arkansas to get it!

The ten-hour drive through Texas
After the hurricane,
Will probably require us
To bring essential things.

I must update my list of meds,
I must take lots of water;
I need some snacks to carry,
And a few things for my daughter.

I need to bring a sweater,
Since the temperature, I've found
In the hospital is freezing cold—
Yet humid all around.

A puzzle book, a novel,
Some note cards and some stamps
May help me pass the waiting time
Beside the reading lamps.

Oh yes! I need my Bible
Or a good devotion book,
To keep my faith and hope strong
And raise my spirits up!

No need to list the clothes I'll pack,
I do that easily,
Since I've been down this path before
A dozen times, you see.

If doubting blurs my vision
That all will be OK,
I'll need to pack some extra faith
To take along the way.

I only need to live today,
Not looking on ahead.
Ingesting life in tiny bites—
That minimizes dread.

Although my daughter's driving,
It's God who steers our way,
As we head down to Houston-town
To check in MDA!

Into the Wind

My three-month checkup was at hand
When Hurricane Harvey struck.
However, we chose to go on,
That we would have good luck.

We wanted to be helpful
In some specific way
To those whose homes had been destroyed
Along its path that day.

So we bought pre-paid credit cards
Of fifty dollars each
To give to those who needed help
Whom we hoped we would meet.

We didn't know what damage
The hurricane had wreaked
When Harvey had preceded us
In fury the past week.

When entering the city,
It surprised us that the water
Had disappeared completely
And things looked quite unaltered.

No water lines, no sand bags,
No lakes beside the way--
It all appeared quite normal
To us at dusk that day.

The next day we had testing,
And as we met each nurse,
We asked if they had flooded,
Or something even worse.

The phlebotomist had lost her home,
She said, without a tear;
So we gave her our first prepaid card
To purchase clothes to wear.

When sitting in the waiting room,
I heard a couple whisper,
Worrying about what might become
Of her now-homeless sister.

So the second card was sent by them
To her in Corpus Christi;
When tears ran down their faces,
My eyes were rather misty.

The one who took my vitals
Said she had lost her home;
And when I gave her the third card,
Her bear hug crushed my bones!

Back at the hotel resting,
I talked to manager, Pete,
Who told me two employees
Were definitely in need.

So one card went to a lady
Who manned the desk at nights;
The fifth card was sent to the laundress
Who works hard out of sight.

As we were in the lobby,
A daughter wheeled in a woman
Whose balding head was proof enough
Of chemo in the moment.

Her lack of hair was evidence
That cancer was within,
But the jaunty cap that covered it
Hid her new-shorn skin.

I offered her my stack of caps
And wigs and hats and such.
Her face lit up, a smile emerged,
With "Thank you very much!"

So heading back to Arkansas,
We felt we'd given hope
To Texans who were scarred by floods,
And maybe helped them cope.

And in return, our hearts were full--
We gained more than we gave!
By sharing with courageous souls
We may have helped to save.

The purpose of our trip, you see,
Was for checkups and testing;
But what we brought back home with us
Were stories full of blessings.

We gained so much by giving,
And that's true every day.
Don't wait to have a hurricane
To see so many ways!

So look around and find them,
And it will warm your heart;
By offering your hand to help,
You'll know you've done your part.

Neuropathy Blues

Neuropathy, neuropathy,
You stole my hands and feet from me!
You say it is a side effect?
Well, it has made my life a wreck!

I wake up with my feet on fire,
Like Joan of Arc upon a pyre!
The only way to get relief
Is walking round on dead man's feet!

How can it hurt, yet be so numb?
And where is the pain coming from?
The chemo left a calling card—
The past few months have been so hard!

My hands that love to draw and paint
Just hurt so much, I know they can
Do arts-and-crafty things no more,
Like what they used to do before.

And then there is the violin
That long ago, I'm not sure when,
Used to sound fluid, the bow moved easy—
Now every stroke can make me queasy.

My cursive is not up to snuff;
The loops and lines are rather rough.
A thank-you note now must be read
With sideways squint and tilted head.

But I'll continue trying hard
To catch neuropathy off-guard
And sneak a painting and a song,
When once my hands can play along!

Then might I also add a dance?
I'll pirouette, I'll clog, perchance;
And I will glide across the floor,
Like none of those who've danced before!

Am I just wishing or just dreaming?
Maybe my mind is only scheming
In order to assuage the pain
Of knowing I won't dance again.

Neuropathy, you're just a trade
For putting cancer in the shade!
I may be sitting out the dance,
But, as for Life, I have a chance!

So thank you, God, for tingly hands,
For numbing feet that cannot stand,
Because they're proof I'm living still,
A fact that is extremely real!

When I decide to paint a bit,
Beside me close, I know You'll sit;
Then, arm and arm, we two will go
To shuffle off to Buffalo!

POSTSCRIPT

This book may have been purchased, because you or someone very close to you has been diagnosed with cancer or another debilitating disease. Life with cancer can be difficult and expensive for both the patients and their caretakers who are forced to juggle treatments and work, without any guarantee of a happily ever after. If you are the patient, the poems may serve as a reminder that you are not alone in how you feel, both physically and emotionally. For a caregiver, the words may help explain what is going on in the mind and body of the patient.

When injecting humor in the poems, my intent was never to sound flippant to the challenges of health or family hardships that cancer entails. Instead, my purpose was to offer assurance that, though the road may be rough, it is still a well-worn path through a difficult time, leading into the future of possibilities.

So, readers, I want to leave you with what I have learned during this year to help you endure the journey as positively as possible:

- Pray. Then pray some more. God is just a prayer away, always listening.
- Be thankful for every blessing, both great and small. In the process, the small miraculously becomes great. Keep a daily gratitude list.
- Be joyful! A smile can be a Roman candle in the darkened sky, a burst of hope to help face the day and let others know they have helped you.
- Be faithful and faith-filled. Read the Bible, devotional books, and self-help books daily, listen to uplifting music,

and watch inspirational movies. Doom and gloom may cloud your skies even more than the illness itself.

- Communicate with others, when you are able. Even a short text or note will give them assurance that their caring for you matters. They need to be replenished with words of heartfelt concern about what's happening in their own lives.

- Don't kick the dog. Some days are harder than others, and those you love the most, who are caring daily for your needs, are usually the ones you may verbally attack when pain or discomfort overwhelms.

- Keep testing your "normal." Once again, pick up the crochet needle, the piano, the paint box, or the golf club, and give it a try. If you don't succeed, it doesn't mean you've failed; it just means you need to allow more time.

- Interact often with the children in your life. Physical and emotional changes may be frightening to them, and they may be uncertain how to react to you at all. They need to know that you are still "you" in their lives.

- Be courteous to those involved in your recuperation, from the medical staff to the workers in the hospital and clinic. A kind word to the person who cleans your hospital room daily will let that person know their job is very important to your recovery.

- Let go of control. God will lead you. Through Him, you will be blessed, comforted, and strengthened.

Gratitude And Grace

As the African proverb says, "It takes a village to raise a child," so is it true that it has taken the sum of so many to get me through my year of cancer and recovery. During the months of solitude, when I shut away the world while I healed, every prayer was felt, every card was treasured, every little gift was my "gold, frankincense, and myrrh," to be taken out countless times to once again experience my humble gratitude at being so loved and supported.

My family all gathered round to help care for me. My husband, Bart, who has been my best friend, constant support, and loving companion for almost half a century, never left my side. Our daughter, Jody, drove us to and from Houston for every hospital visit, as well as religiously conquered the mountain of insurance claims. When work allowed, our son, Woody, came from New York to stay with me in Houston and in Arkansas; and whenever he could not come, he daily checked on my progress by phone, giving me laughter and hope every day. My brother, Robert, flew from Washington, D.C., to be with us whenever he was needed. My niece, Melissa, wrote handwritten letters to me each week, a rare gift in this era of texting. Emma and Garraway, my grandchildren, gave me the strong desire to never give up, so that I can see their life unfold as they mature into adulthood.

Our friends and neighbors were amazing caregivers as well. Patty, a friend since childhood, came from Memphis several times, armed with chicken soup and playing cards. Diana, a friend from Mississippi, kept me spiritually focused through daily prayers, calls, and texts reminding me to "Be still" and that "God is always here." Ruth, a friend from Louisiana, blessed me with audio books, cards, a listening ear, and a Christian example. Sharon, who, through personal experience of cancer in her own family, knows well the path I trod, offered enthusiastic affirmations, heartfelt prayers, anecdotal stories, and plain old common sense. Every time we returned from Houston, a quart of Janet's delicious boiled custard was waiting on my doorstep. The Carmical families, our closest neighbors, not only brought food and flowers, but also shouldered farm chores, such as hauling firewood, feeding the puppy, getting the mail, and even burying our aged family pet during my confinement.

Sissy and Sarah, my sisters in cancer, motivated me with their courage to endure and faith to sustain. John Porter, Bart's hunting buddy, regaled us with stories of hunting and local history when he often stopped by for coffee. Charles fed us with his incredible gifts of music, faith, friendship,--as well as sacks of groceries he often delivered to our back door. He and a former pastor, Jim, served as my spiritual support during that time. A trio of Monticello friends--Susan, Kay, and Mary Jo--showed up at my doorstep to offer healing soup, interesting and inspirational books, and even a can of tuna fish to share. Rose Ann dropped by to bring samples of her delicious hot tamales; and David and Faye regularly sent a variety of meals and snacks--especially on Thanksgiving, when they surprised us with most of our dinner. Andy and Jeff kept the new puppy on our trips to Houston, since she was too little to be boarded. On Facebook, former students and coworkers, as well as others whose paths I have crossed during my seventy years, sent comments and news from their families and the world outside my home. Cards from local churches, community groups, and caring individuals weighed down our mailbox, while lifting my spirits daily.

I was blessed with an amazing medical team as well. Dr. Jack Burge, our family doctor who discovered the tumor in its early stage; and Dr. Pedro Ramirez, my surgeon at MDA, who confirmed the diagnosis, removed the large tumor, and directed the subsequent chemotherapy, literally saved my life. The staff at M D Anderson Gynecology Oncology Department, especially Cheryl and Danielle, kept open communication with us at all times and were always prompt in answering questions that arose.

There are also several talented individuals who helped with the creation of this book. My children, Jody and Woody, with my friends, Sharon, Ruth, and Kay, and Charles, initially read the manuscript rough draft to offer useful suggestions for additions, deletions, and flow. Nancy Potter not only put the photos and cover painting in the correct format for submission, but also gave her expertise on photo placement and citations. Rev. Jim Polk, who had encouraged me throughout my illness to publish the poems, wrote a review for the dust jacket, and Sharon Bale penned a review.

These "dear hearts and gentle people" served as the hands, feet, and heart of God during the year. Like dominoes in a line, each was part of a chain reaction to sustain me steadily onward toward physical and spiritual wellness, as well as completion of the manuscript. For these and all my many blessings, I am most grateful.

The Bynum family at the farm

Although this is Judy's first published book, she previously illustrated and contributed to two published curriculum books and was co-artist of two pen-and-ink calendars of Drew County historical places.

According to her friend, Sharon Bale, "Judy's lifetime of faith, caring for others through her vocational calling in education and interest in the arts, raising two children, caring for a sister in her own battle with cancer and for a parent and a dear friend with Alzheimer's, and thirteen years as a preacher's wife, taught her the many aspects of life-changing illnesses. When her son-in-law and daughter had to relocate to Houston for his bone marrow transplant and chemo treatments for eight months, Judy moved to southern Louisiana to take care of the grandchildren. As her own physical journey with cancer began, sympathy turned into empathy, because she understood it all within her being. Unfortunately, many people who have walked their own journey with cancer do not know how to express the loneliness and pain that is surrounding them. It is for these individuals that Judy felt her poems could help them find their voice."